To Mar... I enjoyed having you in my class. Thanks for coming. Dr Bob

drbob@c3intl.org

GROWTH BY ACCIDENT,
DEATH BY PLANNING

GROWTH BY ACCIDENT, DEATH BY PLANNING

HOW NOT TO KILL A GROWING CONGREGATION

BOB WHITESEL

Abingdon Press/Nashville

GROWTH BY ACCIDENT, DEATH BY PLANNING
HOW NOT TO KILL A GROWING CONGREGATION

Copyright © 2004 by Abingdon Press

This book is printed on acid-free paper.

Library of Congress Cataloging-in-Publication Data

Whitesel, Bob.
  Growth by accident, death by planning : how not to kill a growing congregation / Bob Whitesel.
    p. cm.
  Includes bibliographical references and index.
  ISBN 0-687-08325-7
  1. Church growth. I. Title.

  BV652.25.W487 2004
  254'.5—dc22

2003019628

04 05 06 07 08 09 10 11 12 13—10 9 8 7 6 5 4 3 2 1

MANUFACTURED IN THE UNITED STATES OF AMERICA

CONTENTS

ACKNOWLEDGMENTS

Don't worry about us. This needs to get out. That's thanks enough.
—The pastor of a church in suburban Detroit

With these words our phone conversation was drawing to a close. This pastor had spent several excruciating sessions going over how his church, once with so much potential and growth, was now stalled, even declining in a growing suburb. "Don't use our name . . . but use our mistakes to help others," he concluded.

That was one of many conversations held with pastors of varying church sizes in all sorts of scenarios. All of these pastors shared one thing in common, however. They pastored churches that at one time had been growing, but now often to the pastors' bewilderment, their churches were declining. My first acknowledgment goes out to these honest and forthright church shepherds who helped me understand the planning errors that have stalled and, in many cases, shriveled up once vibrant congregations.

Second, I would like to thank the many church leaders who assisted me in investigating their growing churches and how growth can be sustained even when the community surrounding a church is declining. Certainly, candor is much easier when one leads a growing congregation. But these shepherds bravely let me delve into their personal and church personalities to understand how they avoided the inevitable planning missteps that impede many churches.

I am also grateful to my colleagues in the church leadership and growth field. My mentors have been especially insightful, including C. Peter Wagner, Donald A. McGavran, Eddie Gibbs, and George Hunter. Through their writings and courses, I was tutored to look at the Great Commission (Matt. 28:18-20) not only as a mandate, but also a measurable process.

My academic colleagues helped me build on this foundation, refining and substantiating my theories and research. Kent R. Hunter added an immeasurable amount of support and encouragement, while Kent Miller from Purdue University's Krannert School of Management steered me in new directions of cutting-edge research. Roger Finke and Kevin Dougherty shed light on how economics and sociology greatly shape church planning; and Bruno Dyck honed my understanding of the strategic management process in churches. My associates at Indiana Wesleyan University such as David Wright, Mark Smith, Sharon Drury, Julia Bikel, and Brad Grubb were likewise invaluable as they encouraged me to teach courses on management that defined my theories and gave rise to my research. But most helpful of all may have been my coworkers in the field of church growth consulting. Gary McIntosh, John Baergen, and Ray Ellis were always standing by with encouragement at just the right times. Chip Arn and Steve Wilkes were continually available to mull over my ideas and concepts, and added their insights.

These leaders have unquestionably shaped my professional expertise, but my family has immeasurably shaped me as a person. My lovely wife, Rebecca, who accepted my stammering proposal for marriage in 1973, remains my lifelong confidante, mate, and coworker. And the wonderful offspring of our marriage, Breanna, Kelly, Corrie, and Ashley, remain the joys of my life. As I watch them launch out into careers and testimonies for our Lord, I sense that in these ladies, rather than my writings, may be my legacy.

And finally, my Lord and Savior has beyond a doubt been the greatest source of motivation and encouragement. The gift of new life remains, among all the blessings listed above, the most cherished and treasured. I am thankful that his Spirit has assisted me, along with those I love, and those who have taught me, in becoming a more tenacious as well as a more perceptive Christian.

Dr. Bob Whitesel
Creative Church Consulting Intl.
Winona Lake, IN 46590-0788
www.c3intl.org

INTRODUCTION

If you want to know why a church is growing, don't ask the pastor.
—Donald A. McGavran, missionary and initiator
of the Church Growth Movement[1]

As Yogi Berra famously intoned, "It was déjà vu all over again." Have you ever experienced a word, phrase, or idiom spoken with such familiar expression that suddenly you were swept away to a time long ago? As a church consultant, I heard a recent statement by the young pastor of a rapidly growing congregation that triggered such a recollection.

"I don't know why we are growing. I'm at a loss to explain it," he declared. The Midwestern congregation had grown from one hundred to twenty-five hundred attendees in ten years. Now, on the cusp of purchasing land and building a new facility, the pastor mused about how his lack of knowledge about church planning had not hampered the church's growth to any perceivable degree.

As the pastor ruminated over his predicament, I daydreamed, if but briefly, to a similar scenario almost exactly twenty years earlier and three thousand miles away. On that occasion I had sat in another pastor's office and witnessed the same bewilderment. He was the shepherd of a fast-growing Southern California congregation, and my doctoral facilitator sent me to interview him as part of a research project. "I don't understand why this church is growing," he confided. "People come from all over the world and ask us what we are doing, and I don't know what to tell them. I can't explain it." His words were so similar to my present encounter that on this nearly two-decade anniversary I felt as if I had been swept back to my former experience.

Yet the disturbing thing is that knowledge of how a growing church actually grows (and why it stops growing) was just as elusive and bewildering two decades ago as it is today.

Growing Churches Usually Plateau Too Soon

While interviewing pastors of growing churches, I have found that the pastoral vision for the eventual size of the church usually never materializes. In fact, growing churches seem on average to attain only about half the size of their intentions. Often, this lack of goal attainment begins with a marked slowing of growth and an ensuing plateau. Then, due perhaps to a disappointment in not reaching the stated growth goals, schisms and conflicts may arise to divide the shepherds and sheep into competing offspring.

If these pastoral growth goals are imparted by God, as I believe in most circumstances they are, then these churches plateau too soon. With this in mind, I decided to craft a list of actions that distinguish the growing periods of churches from the customary growth plateau that follows.

Church Growth by Accident:
Unplanned Strategic Decisions

The accompanying chapters are based on my observations that unplanned or "accidental" strategic decisions are often made early on by growing churches, and that these decisions lead to growth. Their leaders employ many of these strategies not because of familiarity with their potential, but because of necessity brought on by the church's circumstances. Thus, these decisions are not planned strategies, but strategies that often occur by accident, owing their genesis to circumstances. These unplanned strategic decisions are driven not by knowledge, but by the church's situation.

As the church grows, the leaders often become perplexed over the causes of this extraordinary growth and seek to uncover causal factors. Because the factors are so elusive and since many church leaders are not trained in the literature and principles of church growth, they may become bewildered. Soon this bewilderment surfaces in sermons and casual conversations, communicating an inner puzzlement over the forces involved. The quotations at the beginning of this introduction are examples of how this concern sometimes surfaces in pastoral interviews.

Church Death by Planning: Looking at Others Rather Than Looking at Ourselves

Eventually and typically, the leaders of the growing church begin to read church growth books, periodicals, and case studies. Often the leaders make strategic planning decisions that are similar to those of other churches they perceive to be in their situation. Because the majority of larger churches have adopted strategic plans that have plateaued their congregations, the growing church follows suit. And herein rise the factors that inhibit growth.

Our Future May Lie in Our Past

My belief is that planning is not wrong; rather, the problem comes with planning that does not fully understand the factors that contributed to growth in the first place.

To help the church leader visualize these planning missteps (and their corrective actions), I have created figure A: "Why Growing Churches Plateau: And What You Can Do About It." This figure will serve as a pattern for the eleven chapters, each of which will include the following:

1. factors that cause initial growth in churches,
2. erroneous decisions that lead to plateauing, and
3. corrective steps to regain growth that are more in keeping with the factors that contributed to growth in the first place.

Let's Not Forget the Holy Spirit's Participation

Before we undertake our list, let me acknowledge in the strongest terms the role of the Holy Spirit in all church growth. Because church growth is first and foremost a work of the Holy Spirit (John 16:8-9), no real and enduring growth can occur without the Holy Spirit's participation. Granted, some churches briefly grow by purely secular plans and processes, but the churches to which I am referring are those that have God's unseen hand of blessing clearly upon them. As a result, I believe this unseen hand has led them to employ certain fundamental and God-derived principles that have resulted in growth. And thus, I cannot stress too highly the indispensable nature of the Holy Spirit's participation in growth.

However, in this book I will focus on the fashionable strategies that often replace the God-derived tactics that contributed to growth.

The Third Part of a Three-Book Series

This book is the third in a series on growing a healthy and effective multi-generational church. Although it is certainly not necessary to read the two earlier books to derive insight and value from this present volume, the earlier books build a foundation for the planning steps outlined here.[2] Together, all three books describe a comprehensive, simple, and field-tested strategy for growing a healthy congregation.

A User-friendly Structure for Each Chapter

To help the reader quickly assimilate the information in each chapter, I have created the following structure. Each chapter is structured around six subtopics:

1. Each chapter begins with a story of a growing church that plateaued.[3]

2. "Factors That Cause Initial Growth" (column one in figure A) will then be investigated.

3. "Erroneous Decisions That Lead to Plateauing" (column two in figure A) will be described.

4. "Corrective Steps to Regain Initial Growth" (column three in figure A) will be analyzed and illustrated.

5. Each chapter will conclude with another example, this time of an actual church that did not plateau but continued growing.

6. An addendum to each chapter titled "Questions for Group Study" will help leaders apply to their situation the lessons learned in each chapter.

The Message Was There All Along—from McGavran

The quote by Donald A. McGavran in the epigraph signaled that even years ago, it was known that the elusive nature of church growth escapes most pastors. In his classes on church growth at Fuller Seminary, McGavran was famous for his observation: "If you want to know why a church is growing, don't ask the pastor." Many of us heard this adage, noted its appropriateness, and then filed it away somewhere in the recesses of our minds while the electrifying topics of spiritual gifts, power evangelism, cell groups, and celebrations commanded our attention. Granted, these more stirring subjects were basics of solid and healthy church structure, and should not be ignored. But in our enthusiasm, sometimes the more provocative principles overshadowed the more mundane (and potentially more critical) axioms.

Hundreds of church leaders were trained under Dr. McGavran's tutelage. In almost every seminary and sizable city you will find leaders who fondly remember the principles that McGavran so gregariously intoned. However, one of McGavran's most important lessons may have been lost in the clamor over more celebrated principles. Donald McGavran's observation, that the shepherd may be the last to correctly perceive what has led to growth (and by inference what will stop it), may be one of the most important teachings of that sprightly professor with the gray goatee.

The clue to what can stop churches from growing—it may have been there all along.

Figure A: Why Growing Churches Plateau: And What You Can Do About It

Factors That Cause Initial Growth in Churches	Erroneous Decisions That Lead to Plateauing	Corrective Steps to Regain Initial Growth
Chapter 1. Focus is on meeting the needs of the congregants and the community.	Focus is increasingly on the needs of a burgeoning staff, comprised of experienced volunteers and professional workers.	Make planning decisions based upon congregational and community needs (using surveys, focus groups, personal interaction, etc.), not on the conveniences of the staff (which are usually expressed more vocally and assertively than congregational needs).
Chapter 2. Celebration Convenience: multiple church celebrations are held at varying times and/or venues.	Waning Celebration Convenience: celebrations are combined in larger facilities and at fewer times. As a result fewer options are offered for congregants and community residents (but convenience increases for the staff).	Maintain as many celebrations as feasible in order to offer as many convenient worship times and styles as possible.
Chapter 3. Urgency in prayer is due to potential for failure. Also, a significant portion of the prayer focus is on the unchurched and dechurched. (*Dechurched* is defined as "those who have terminated their attendance elsewhere due to some real or perceived hurt, conflict, etc.")	Security in circumstances robs prayer of its urgency. Prayer focus is also increasingly on the needs of church attendees rather than on dechurched and unchurched people. In addition, institutionalization of prayer takes place. Prayer forms are standardized and formalized, especially in the church celebration.	Don't wait for a crisis to reinvigorate the prayer life of a church. Consider the enormity and significance of the task you are undertaking: the Great Commission (Matt. 28:18-20). Also, employ 50/50 prayer, where 50% of the prayer focus is on congregational needs while the other 50% addresses the needs of the unchurched and dehurched.

Chapter 4. Budget is structured and conservative, primarily based on money in hand.	Budgeting is overly optimistic, based upon the euphoria of initial growth. In the name of flexibility the structure of the budgeting process may also be scrapped. If growth slows, fiscal flexibility will tighten quickly and dramatically, often leading to conflict and tension.	Budget more conservatively and more intentionally than you feel you should. Church leaders are often optimists, but basing budgets on overly optimistic projections or eschewing budget procedures in the name of flexibility can be reckless.
Chapter 5. Rented or renovated facilities are cost-effective, flexible, and multi-functional.	Dramatic increase in overhead is due to newly purchased or constructed facilities. In addition, these facilities are often segregated into activity-specific spaces (i.e., immovable pews in an auditorium, small Sunday school rooms that cannot open up into larger quarters, etc.).	Utilize the "Seven Dos When Building a Facility" outlined in chapter 5, including renting or remaining longer than you think you need to. Doing this will place hardship upon your staff, but increase your financial viability and future flexibility. Also, create flexibiltiy in your facilities. Then when it is time to build, employ architects who build malls, colleges, and theaters, not those who primarily build churches.
Chapter 6. Experimentation is encouraged. Almost all theologically theologically noncompromising ideas are considered.	The church begins to stay with "what has worked in the past," even if that is the immediate past. This often leads to incipient traditionalism.	Foster an environment of experimentation and exploration. Rapid changes in cultural predilections and preferences require this.
Chapter 7. Housecleaning occurs. Ideas that don't work are quickly abandoned. Limited resources and the precariousness of the church's survival create this situation.	Programs and ideas that may not be productive are given extra time "to develop." Jesus' parable on repentance (Luke 13:1-9) is often misapplied to rationalize extending the life of an unproductive program.	Be prepared to use vigorous analysis and empirical evidence to confirm productive programming. Often supporting evidence of a program's viability is anecdotal. Look for clear evidence of productivity (James 3:17).

Chapter 8. Dysfunctional people become functional. All people, regardless of physical, social, or economic dysfunction, are actively recruited. Prior leadership experience in another church is not required.	Functionally adept people are actively recruited. Prior leadership experience in another church is highly valued. Unproductive programming is often unintentionally cross-pollinated.	Utilize small groups and a lay-training system to mentor dysfunctional people into functional and productive lives in both church and society.
Chapter 9. Staff members have low educational experience in their ministry fields. Thus, they do what they intuitively "sense" or "feel" is right. Plus, new ideas are generated from the constituency they serve.	Staff members become trained in the "classical" fields of theology, Christian education, church music, and ministry. These newly acquired skills are probably those that are practiced in influential but plateaued churches. In addition, new ideas are increasingly generated from professional colleagues instead of constituents.	Embrace 50/50 learning. Learning engendered in the "classical" milieu of seminaries, workshops, and Bible colleges must be balanced by 50% of the learning coming from practical and alternative sources, such as nonaccredited institutes (e.g., the Wagner Institute), workshops, field experience, and secular opportunities.
Chapter 10. Small groups are not yet essential. The church's growth is driven by the "event status" of the celebration.	Small groups, though necessary to foster intimacy, are not sufficiently developed because the "event status" of the worship celebration continues to drive the church's emphasis and reputation. Because intimacy is missing, people feel the church is "too cold" or "not personal enough," and they go elsewhere.	Establish an extensive network of small groups to maintain intimacy and commitment as the church grows. Develop all types of small groups, including adult Sunday school classes, leadership teams, home groups, ministry groups, interest groups, organic groups, and so forth.
Chapter 11. Due to conviction, the magnitude of the task, and potential for failure, Christ recognized as the focal point of the church's mission and empowerment.	Along with growth comes a variety of potentials, pressures, and problems whose perceived magnitude begins to subtly dwarf the primacy of Christ.	Stay rooted in the Word, prayer, ministry, accountability, and one's mortality to keep Christ central in the lives and ministries of the is congregants and leaders.

CHAPTER 1

Missteps with Staff Influence

Service is the rent that you pay for room on this earth.
—Shirley Chisholm, African American congresswoman[1]

Factors That Cause Initial Growth in Churches	Erroneous Decisions That Lead to Plateauing	Corrective Steps to Regain Initial Growth
Focus is on meeting the needs of the congregants and the community.	Focus is increasingly on the needs of a burgeoning staff, comprised of experienced volunteers and professional workers.	Make planning decisions based upon congregational and community needs (discovered through surveys, focus groups, personal interaction, etc.), not on the conveniences of the staff (which are usually expressed more vocally and assertively than congregational needs).

Growing Away from Your Roots

"We aren't the church we used to be. We're in Mendellville, but we act like we're in Southtown. No wonder we've stopped growing."

"They could have asked me," quipped Marty, the head usher of a new church recently started two blocks from Mendellville Church (a pseudonym). "Mendellville Church once really understood this neighborhood," continued Marty. "Now they're just like those people in Southtown. Is it any wonder that's where they're going?"

Southtown was a growing suburb, less than four miles away, but light-years away economically from Mendellville. Mendellville was a small community nestled along the river of a growing city of 65,000. Originally home to Ukrainian immigrants, in recent years Mendellville had enjoyed an influx of Hispanic families attracted by the affordable housing. And though annexed by the city some forty years ago, Mendellville had winding streets and thickly wooded hills that helped it preserve the feeling of a distinct community.

Only eight years earlier, Mendellville Church had been a declining congregation. But the hiring of an energetic new pastor named Serge inaugurated growth. Of Hispanic extraction, Serge led the church into a strong growth cycle, and soon the church was exploring the possibility of constructing new facilities.

At that time I was hired to help the church plan its future. However, as I analyzed the growth patterns, a disturbing trend came to my attention. The growth at Mendellville Church had been slowing and had almost reached a standstill. The small group network, outreach strategies, assimilation programs, facilities, and other key church growth components did not appear to be the culprits. Yet as I probed deeper, I discovered that an informal, but persistent exodus of attendees had been taking place over the past two years. Emmanuel Church, of which Marty was the head usher, was the most recent unplanned offspring of Mendellville Church. And thus, Serge encouraged me to start my investigation there.

A series of interviews with Emmanuel's leaders revealed that they held an impression that as Mendellville Church grew, its leaders became less in touch with the needs of the neighborhood and the congregants. "They were part of the neighborhood when they began," remembered George, a member of Emmanuel Church. "But as they got big, so did their heads."

Trying to defuse the comment, Marty interrupted, "It's not that they didn't care about the Lord. It's just that they seemed to be less concerned about the problems in this community and more concerned about the problems of running a big church. When a lot of the leaders moved to Southtown, that just made it worse."

Southtown was a growing suburb nearby, with quiet streets, upper-middle-class housing, and good schools. Many Hispanic businessowners and professionals had made it their home, often moving from Mendellville. As I continued the interviews with Emmanuel's leaders, it became clear they felt that Mendellville Church's leaders had subtly shifted their focus from the needs of the congregants to the needs of a staff that was climbing the socioeconomic ladder.

I summarized these observations in a letter to Serge. When we met two weeks later, I prepared for some tension, if not outright disagreement. "You have understood this exactly," began Serge. "We aren't the church we used to be. We're in Mendellville, but we act like we're in Southtown. No wonder we've stopped growing." As we continued our conversation, Serge recalled incident after incident where the staff's wishes and needs had taken precedence over the needs of the neighborhood constituency. "I guess we grew away from our roots," summarized Serge. "That's a horrible thing to do."

Factors That Caused Initial Growth

Over the next three months, I worked with the church leaders to uncover some of the causal factors for the growth and the ensuing plateau of Mendellville Church. The following were some of the most notable:

Cause of Growth #1: The church reached out to the community's changing ethnicity. When Serge became the pastor of

Mendellville Church, he was the first Hispanic pastor in the church's history. Previously a community of Ukrainian immigrants, Mendellville had developed over the years into a predominantly Hispanic neighborhood. Recognizing this, the leaders of the church hired a talented Hispanic pastor to reach out to the community. Gerald, a former leader of Mendellville Church who was of Ukrainian descent, remembered, "We hired Ukrainian pastors for years to reach the neighborhood. Why shouldn't we hire a Hispanic pastor now?" He was right, for there was no compelling rationale not to.

Cause of Growth #2: The church instituted a leadership development program to train indigenous leaders. As the church began to grow, it was desperate for leaders. Serge launched a lay-training institute to develop leaders from the community. This clear route into leadership attracted many people who otherwise might not have considered leadership due to inexperience and/or apprehension.

Cause of Growth #3: The church leaders were in touch with the needs of the community. Because the leaders of Mendellville Church lived and usually worked in the community, they understood it intuitively. "I lived in the parsonage for five years," recalled Serge. "And you can't help getting to know a lot of people in Mendellville when your home is thirty feet from the church."

Cause of Growth #4: Any willing community resident could become involved in leadership. A pressing need for leaders forced the church to utilize almost any willing volunteer. This approach will be discussed in greater detail in chapter 8. But here suffice it to say that anyone, regardless of skill or background, could try his or her hand at almost any leadership responsibility. This not only created new and innovative ministries, but also bolstered the self-esteem of congregants.

Cause of Growth #5: The leaders inaugurated innovative ministries that met the community needs. The result of Causes of Growth #2 to #4 was that the church launched ministries that effectively and creatively addressed the needs of community residents.

Erroneous Decisions That Led to Plateauing

The future looked bright for Mendellville Church, but as the congregation experienced growth, the leaders unintentionally and often unknowingly began to distance themselves from the constituency they served. Here are some of the erroneous decisions that contributed to this growing gulf and eventually plateaued Mendellville Church.

Error 1: Leaders slowly became isolated from the average congregant. With the growth and success of the church, which in five years numbered more than 450 in attendance, a slow distancing of the staff from the average attendee took place. Many of the staff enjoyed incomes almost 60 percent more than what they had received five years before. And many moved to Southtown and other nearby middle-income communities. As a result, the staff had less and less daily contact with Mendellville residents. Though the staff served in the community, they no longer lived in the community.

Error 2: Leaders relied more on their past experiences to guide them rather than on current circumstances. Management researchers David Dotlich and Peter Cairo have discovered that as leaders climb the ladder of success, they begin to distance themselves from those they serve and fall victim to the "experience trap."[2] This trap arises when a leader, increasingly detached from the needs of his or her constituency, begins to rely more and more on past experience for guidance. However, these past experiences are becoming antiquated, and leaders become less innovative and creative because they are caught in an outdated, but comfortable, "experience trap."

Error 3: A minority began to resent the majority because it seemed that 20 percent of the congregation was doing 80 percent of the work. A burgeoning congregation meant increasing pressure was put on the staff. Italian economist Vilfredo Pareto is famed for his observation that "80% of the value lies in 20% of the elements, while the remaining 20% of the value lies in the remaining 80% of the elements."[3] This adage has been used anecdotally to imply that 80 percent of the volunteer work in a church is undertaken by 20 percent of the volunteers. And often, something near this percentage is the case. In the Mendellville Church, the 20 percent or so who assumed the majority of the work began to reach a stage of burnout. And this emotional exhaustion often led to disparaging remarks about the uninvolved 80 percent. Though these comments were tendered in jest, they signaled a growing rift between the leaders and the people they served.

Error 4: Experience was preferred over willingness. This error will surface again in chapter 8 as a culprit behind early plateaus in growth. However, it also occurs here, for as the church grew in stature, its duties also seemed to grow in importance. "It seemed harder to trust inexperienced people with tasks in the church because so much was riding on it," remembered Serge. As a result, a subtle, almost imperceptible, professionalization of the paid and volunteer staff took place.

Error 5: Staff concerns carried more weight than congregational concerns. As the staff grew, so did their clout. Increasingly insulated from the average congregant, they assumed their needs mirrored the needs of the neighborhood. And when it was time to make decisions, the staff's input carried a disproportionate amount of weight. "The staff were the ones lobbying for a move to Southtown," recalled Serge. "It's closer to where most of us now live." The effect of staff preferences upon church relocation will be investigated further in chapter 5.

Error 6: Clashes between leaders began to receive more attention than the clash between community residents and secular culture. As Mendellville Church grew, subtle fiefdoms developed among various programs. When the church crossed the 200 attendance barrier, its orientation became what Gary McIntosh calls "programmatic in orientation."[4] In other words, the programs and their staffing, space, and fiscal needs began to seize the church's attention. In a milieu of increasing but still limited funds, each ministry begin to fight over resources. The result was polarization, with some segments of the church coalescing into identifiable factions. And when a church passes the 400 attendance barrier, McIntosh points out the orientation will begin to focus on administration.[5] As a result, a further estrangement among factions took place due to disagreements over systems and styles of administration. Subsequently, conflicts among the leaders took a disproportionate amount of the church's energy, time, and focus. The community, engaged in a battle with secularizing culture, failed to garner sufficient attention from church leaders embroiled in battles between fiefdoms.

Corrective Steps to Regain Growth

Ten Steps to Staying Connected to the People You Serve

To regain growth, church leaders must recognize their inclination to become isolated from their constituency and then undertake corrective steps to reverse this disconnect.

Corrective Step #1: Stay connected with your congregation by living among them. Though the rising social and economic stature of a congregation may allow its leaders to move up the socioeconomic ladder and out of the local community, leaders must seriously consider the benefits of residing among their constituents. Jesus modeled this behavior, choosing to eat and fellowship among society's disadvantaged, much to the annoyance of the religious elite (Mark 2:15-16).

Corrective Step #2: Stay connected by visiting small groups within the church. Chapter 10 points out that much of the accountability and candor of a congregation takes place in small groups. As for the present discussion, leaders should regularly visit small group environments to stay connected. Participants will feel more comfortable sharing their concerns and needs in these small groups.

Corrective Step #3: Stay connected with your church newcomers. Guests and visitors can give you a perspective on how well you are competing with the distractions of a secularizing culture. And newcomers do not have the historical baggage that sometimes makes people guard their words and their true feelings. One component is a five-week newcomer course, which allows newcomers to experience a small group environment with other newcomers.[6] This course is an ideal venue for leaders to interact with those new to the congregation and/or Christianity.

Corrective Step #4: Be a servant leader, ready to partake in even the most mundane (and perhaps distasteful) tasks. "One of the things people don't like to do around here is wash the dishes that come back from our weekly dinner at the downtown homeless shelter. You should have seen their faces when they caught me washing them. I do it once a month now," confided Serge. Throughout the Gospels, we are reminded that Jesus, God in the flesh, dutifully and happily modeled the behavior of a servant. His washing of his disciples' feet was the ultimate example, one that stunned Peter in its deference and humility (John 13:1-17). Leaders who stay in touch with their constituents will not find it beneath themselves to model servant leadership even in the most mundane or unpleasant tasks. "Never ask a person to do something you wouldn't do yourself" is a famous adage. For a Christian leader, it might be better expressed, "Never ask a person to do something you haven't modeled yourself."

Corrective Step #5: Evaluate the effectiveness and appropriateness of the church's ministries on a regular basis. This should be accomplished via anecdotal insights and empirical investigation. Chapter 7 is devoted to addressing the important task of evaluation in more detail.[7]

Corrective Step #6: Poll the opinions of the congregation and the community to stay connected. Surveys, town hall meetings, and focus groups can be helpful in uncovering needs and concerns of both the congregation and the community. Let's look briefly at each:

- *Congregational or community questionnaires* can be highly beneficial if they are well designed and permit anonymity. Questionnaires are good gauges of opinions and needs.[8]

- *Town hall meetings* should be conducted at least twice a year in a congregation, and when warranted in a community, to assess opinions and needs. Some denominations already have these structures in place due to democratic forms of church government. However, for those that do not, a meeting modeled after ones convened in the town halls of early America can be invaluable. Certain guide-lines, such as *Robert's Rules of Order*, should be followed to prevent these gatherings from digressing into griev-ance sessions. If care is taken to engender a spirit of con-sideration and openness, these venues can be important places for discovering needs.

- *Focus groups* are small groups convened to direct think-ing toward a particular topic. Similar to town hall meet-ings, only smaller, these groups of three to twelve individuals allow reticent and/or reserved participants to share their thoughts in a more intimate environment.[9]

Corrective Step #7: Develop leaders from your neighbor-hood. While the temptation will be to utilize professionally trained staff as well as lay leaders experienced with large churches, oftentimes such staff will be out of touch with the needs and spirit of the community. Chapter 9, "Missteps with Staff Education," addresses this in detail. However, for the pres-ent discussion, remember that a leader developed from the neigh-borhood will bring a long history of familiarity with the needs and preferences of that community.

Corrective Step #8: Beware of the "Absalom at the Gate Syndrome." The previous steps are essential for remaining aware of community and congregational needs. But they can also lead, sometimes deviously, to more division. In the process of gathering information from congregants and community residents, it will be tempting to politic or champion one's personal solutions and ideas. Leading conversations and/or interjecting personal solutions may undermine information gathering. Remember that King David's son Absalom cunningly sat at the city gate to politic for his father's overthrow (2 Sam. 15:1-12). Leaders must be careful not to suc-cumb to this syndrome. When gathering information on the needs of the congregation and community, suppress your desires and predilections. You are there to learn, not to politic or polarize.

Corrective Step #9: Have an accountability group that can warn you of impending disconnection. In the business world, organizations recognized for their ethical behavior tend to have outside directors who, as independent voices, give advice and counsel. This is necessary because the human tendency to surround oneself with devotees and aficionados can undermine judgment and discernment. Be wary of environments where most decisions are based largely upon the advice of closely connected individuals rather than a broad spectrum of the people you serve, joined by outside voices.

Corrective Step #10: Pray for a humble and sensitive spirit. In Isaiah 66:2, God declares, "This is the one I esteem: he who is humble and contrite in spirit, and trembles at my word." This passage reminds us that God honors and empowers those who build their leadership upon a biblical foundation that is accompanied by compassion and humility.

A SUCCESS STORY

North Coast Church, Vista, California: How to Avoid Being Sucked into the Middle

Larry Osborne is the senior pastor of North Coast Church, a congregation affiliated with the Evangelical Free Church of America, which averages 5,500 attendees in thirteen worship options. I asked Larry, "What do you do to stay connected to the average congregant's needs and wishes as the church grows?"

"There are a number of things that I do to stay in touch," began Larry. "First, I make it a high priority to know the world of people who aren't employed by churches. A lot of pastors know the spiritual and denominational world, but don't know their congregants' world. One way I've addressed this is to read a lot of business and secular journals, things like *Fast Company, Inc., Business 2.0, Time, Newsweek,* and *U.S. News & World Report.* If I don't understand the business world, when a businessperson talks to me about his or her world, it's like we're using two different dictionaries. A lot of businesspeople are shocked to find out that I understand inventory control, tax laws, and can read a balance sheet.

"A second point is that I do everything I can to keep from being 'sucked into the middle.' Leaders get isolated. I call it being sucked into the middle of the organization and away from the people on the edges. It's in the middle where the best and the worst people reside. As the organization grows, I could easily find myself dealing only with the most committed and the most troubled—losing touch with regular people. The fact is, the most important things in our church are happening around the fringe, with regular people. And so, over the years, I have done a variety of things to keep from being sucked into the middle.

"I host welcome desserts at my home where people can meet me somewhere else besides church. We introduce ourselves, I share a five-minute talk about the church, then we just chat. I always ask, 'Why did you come to North Coast the first time?' and 'What brought you through the doors the second time?' It's a very powerful tool for getting information firsthand rather than through an impersonal questionnaire.

"I also teach our pastor's class where I share the vision with newcomers. It's another great opportunity to meet people who are new and to hear their challenges, concerns, and hopes.

"And I try to rub shoulders with people on the fringe by being accessible. Anyone can schedule an appointment with me. And on weekends I walk around among our thirteen worship venues. This way I can see for myself what's happening, plus I learn a great deal by talking to people in the corridors and halls.

"And third, I use what I call 'fast feedback loops.' Our congregation is built around small groups. And each group fills out a short synopsis detailing what happened in the gathering. I personally read all these synopses. After each service, I read every response card that contains a prayer request or question. These actions give me fast feedback from regular folks, and as a result, I don't have to depend on someone else's evaluation. I see each comment or prayer request with my own eyes. I handle it. I touch it. We're too large for me to know everyone, but with these 'fast feedback loops' I can get to know the needs of people on the fringe, not just the middle.

"All of these things help me to know their world, maintain fast feedback, and keep from becoming a prisoner of the middle. Then, I'm ready for ministry."

QUESTIONS FOR GROUP STUDY

The following questions are for group study. Ask yourself each question, and then return to the appropriate corrective steps in this chapter to plan your action steps.

1. Is there a *physical gap* growing between your leaders and their constituency? Is it evident in

   • Leaders moving out of the area?
   • Leaders working outside the area?
   • Leaders only physically in the neighborhood when involved in church business?

2. Is there a *cultural gap* growing between your leaders and their constituency? Ask yourself the following questions:

   • Are your leaders of a different *economic culture* from the majority of the congregation? And are the salaries of your leaders within a 10 percent range (higher or lower) from the median income of your congregation?
   • Are your leaders of a different *social culture* from the majority of the congregation? Ask yourself: Do your leaders socialize, associate, and fraternize differently and/or in different environs than most of the congregants?

3. Do your leaders feel that 20 percent of the congregation is doing 80 percent of the work? Do your leaders feel increasingly burned out? And do your leaders, even subtly, make joking or sarcastic remarks about the uninvolved 80 percent? Could this be contributing to a growing gulf between the two groups? Why or why not?

4. Do clashes between staff and/or programming seem to be taking an increasingly disproportionate amount of the church's time, energy, and fiscal resources? What does this indicate? And what should you do about it?

5. Which voices carry the most clout regarding decisions for your congregation?

   - Are there independent voices that are regularly heard? If so, what does this mean?

   - Is there a tight-knit association of individuals who control a disproportionate amount of the decision-making power? If so, what are the drawbacks to this approach? And what should be done?

CHAPTER 2

Missteps with Worship Celebrations

Variety's the very spice of life,
That gives it all its flavour.

—William Cowper, British poet[1]

Factors That Cause Initial Growth in Churches	Erroneous Decisions That Lead to Plateauing	Corrective Steps to Regain Initial Growth
Celebration Convenience: multiple church celebrations are held at varying times and/or venues.	Waning Celebration Convenience: celebrations are combined in larger facilities and at fewer times. As a result fewer options are offered for congregants and community residents (but convenience increases for the staff).	Maintain as many celebrations as feasible in order to offer as many convenient worship times and styles as possible.

How Mishandling Worship Celebrations Can Stall Growth

"Soon after merging our services, our attendance began deteriorating, . . . that's why we haven't been able to meet our budget."

Scarcely two years had passed since the new sanctuary had been built. It sat adjacent to a major highway, its cream-colored walls tastefully decorated with three inlaid crosses. After church, Bill, the pastor, and Carl, a layman, gathered with me in the front pew of Westside Church. The last time I saw them was two years ago at the dedication of the new sanctuary, and at that time they looked decidedly more optimistic.

"Carl's been doing an analysis on our church attendance because we've lost more than 750 people in the last two years," began Bill. "And he thinks he knows the cause."

Carl, an accountant, continued the thought: "Soon after merging our services, our attendance began deteriorating, and now it's down 31 percent in the last two years."

Bill concluded, "That's why we haven't been able to meet our budget for the past five quarters."

Carl and Bill discovered that after building a new sanctuary and combining worship services, church attendance had temporarily grown, briefly plateaued, and was now in substantial decline.

Factors That Caused Initial Growth

The cause for these attendance swings began to emerge. The first clue surfaced when Carl compared the number of worship services before and after the opening of the new sanctuary.

Prior to constructing the new sanctuary, the congregation had been growing steadily for more than five years. The former sanctuary seated only 750, and each time as it filled, additional services were added. Figure 2.1 describes how growth drove and modified the worship schedule.

Worship celebrations at Westside Church were identical in format, and since the philosophy of ministry was to reach younger generations moving into the nearby suburbs, the church embraced modern music and an informal style.[2]

The proliferation of worship times offered four advantages, which in turn helped drive growth:

Figure 2.1 Weekend Worship Celebrations at Westside Church. Services that were added are outlined .

BEFORE growth began	YEAR 1 of growth	YEARS 2-3 of growth	YEAR 4 of growth	YEAR 5 of growth
Celebration 1: SUNDAY 10:15 A.M. Sunday school at 9:00 A.M.	**Celebration 1:** SUNDAY 8:45 A.M. Sunday school at 10:00 A.M.	**Celebration 1:** SUNDAY 8:45 A.M. Sunday school at 10:00 A.M.	**Celebration 1:** SUNDAY 8:45 A.M. Sunday school at 10:00 A.M.	**Celebration 1:** SUNDAY 8:30 A.M. Sunday school concurrently
	Celebration 2: SUNDAY 11:00 A.M.	**Celebration 2:** SUNDAY 11:00 A.M.	**Celebration 2:** SUNDAY 11:00 A.M.	**Celebration 2:** SUNDAY 9:50 A.M. Sunday school concurrently
		Celebration 3: SATURDAY 5:30 P.M. No Saturday school	**Celebration 3:** SATURDAY 5:30 P.M. Saturday school concurrently	**Celebration 3:** SUNDAY 11:10 A.M. No Sunday school
			Celebration 4: SATURDAY 7:00 P.M. No Saturday school	**Celebration 4:** SATURDAY 5:30 P.M. Saturday school concurrently
				Celebration 5: SATURDAY 7:00 P.M. Saturday school concurrently

Cause of Growth #1: Multiple worship times meant a greater percentage of the community could find suitable times to attend. "We came here because they had a worship service that fit our hectic schedule," confided a thirty-something mother of two. "My husband and I looked around a lot before we found something that fit." More worship alternatives meant a larger segment of the community could find a suitable opportunity to attend Westside Church.

Cause of Growth #2: The same sermon was preached at all services, thus strengthening the church's unity. The services were identical, including the sermon. Thus, attendees could pick a worship service that fit their personal but varying schedule without missing the message other congregants were receiving. As a result, a unified message helped drive growth.

Cause of Growth #3: Each time the auditorium neared capacity, another service was launched, preventing overcrowding from thwarting growth. Peter Wagner described sanctuary overcrowding as "sociological strangulation," since overcapacity can choke off growth.[3] Wagner believes that once the auditorium is 80 percent full, the church has begun to strangle its growth by overcrowding.[4] But diehard regulars are not the ones who are driven away; rather, it is newcomers who each week must wrangle for seating while navigating crowded halls and unfamiliar parking lots.

Cause of Growth #4: New service times relieved congestion in the parking lot. The leaders didn't recognize it at the time, but the parking lots had become overly congested until new celebrations were added. Rarely do leaders peruse the parking situation immediately before worship services, probably because leaders are busy at those times. But when Westside Church multiplied its worship options, it added surplus parking for each service. Some may wonder whether parking is an important consideration. But Robert Schuller argues that modern Americans have become accustomed to the convenience of ample parking, noting "as they have become spoiled by easy parking afforded by the shopping centers, they have become more and more disenchanted, impatient and irritated by the parking congestion they find elsewhere, including that in their own church settings."[5] Though mature Christians should not chaff at parking at inconvenient distances, most will agree that guests and unchurched people can be put off by overly congested parking areas.

Erroneous Decisions That Led to Plateauing

Since Westside Church's three Sunday services attracted a total of 1,770 worshipers, the architect suggested the congregation build a sanctuary that could seat 2,500. The new sanctuary would provide over 40 percent more seating than the *combined* Sunday attendance. They figured they could offer one combined service on Sunday morning and Saturday evening. "The idea was driven by the staff," remembered Bill. "They felt it was a drain on our leaders to hold five weekend services, and they wanted just two."

Subsequently, they made the following missteps:

Error 1: Combining services decreased the number of options for attendees and community residents. Decreasing options can mean that a significant segment of regular as well as potential attendees will find the new times inconvenient and/or impossible. While these attitudes may be somewhat immature, the many newcomers attracted to the church—a sizable portion of the existing attendees—struggled with service times that were less convenient and less attractive.

Error 2: The impetus to combine services was driven largely by the staff. Though the staff was increasing in burnout, it was also increasing in clout. In chapter 1 we saw that as a church grows, the needs of the staff can inadvertently take precedence over the needs of the congregants. The predilection of the staff to voice and lobby for their needs, and a slow distancing of the staff from the average congregant, meant that combining services, though expeditious for the leaders, only increased a sense of inconvenience and disconnection for the average or potential attendee.

Let's take a look at figure 2.2 and see how reducing the number of worship options correlated to a decline in attendance.

Figure 2.2 Attendance before and after fewer service options were offered at Westside Church.

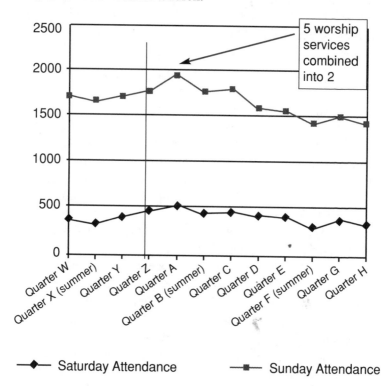

—◆— Saturday Attendance   —■— Sunday Attendance

Figure 2.2 exhibits the short-term attendance "bump" that often coincides with new or remodeled facilities. In most cases this increase will not be maintained. Causal factors include the "new-ness bump," where people check out the "next big thing," but are often disappointed when churches are not prepared for the influx. Usually within six months the church will return to near its prior attendance levels, as Westside did (figure 2.2). Westside Church continued to decline over the next eight quarters, –39 percent and –29 percent in its Saturday and Sunday celebrations, respectively.

Certainly, there were other factors (as there always are) that contributed to growth and decline at Westside Church. Yet no other significant church growth illnesses were evident or discovered. In hindsight, Carl and Bill had concluded that the attendance decline was fueled by a reduction in the options and flexibility that the multiple service format had offered.

Corrective Steps to Regain Growth

Six Steps to Offering the Appropriate Number
of Worship Options

At first glance the prescription may seem to be to add more services. A closer look will reveal that there are important nuances and subtleties to adding celebrations. Let's look at six corrective steps that will help you offer the appropriate number and type of worship options.

Corrective Step #1: Build your celebration strategy on your "philosophy of ministry." There has been some confusion about what constitutes a mission statement, a vision statement, and a philosophy of ministry. Here is a brief overview:

- *A mission statement* is a "broad general statement" of the "basic stance of the church and its intentions," which many churches can share.[6] "To seek and save the lost" would be an example, for many churches could embrace this mission.
- *A vision statement* is "a clear mental image of a preferable future imparted by God and based on an accurate understanding of God, self, and circumstances."[7] This can be summarized as "Where do we believe God is calling our church to go?"[8]
- *A philosophy of ministry* is a comprehensive description of the unique "personality" of a church, and often reaches several pages in length. Kent Hunter's book, *Your Church Has Personality*, is a valuable introduction to writing a philosophy of ministry.[9] Once this description of your church's personality is drafted, you can check to see whether your activities are lining up. At Westside Church part of its philosophy of ministry was "to reach unchurched and dechurched people with innovative presentations of the good news." Thus, Westside placed a higher priority on influencing the community with

the good news than on internal unanimity. Some churches may elevate unity above outreach, but Charles Arn argues that they will have difficulty adding new services.[10]

Therefore, having multiple service options fit Westside's personality and allowed it to affect a greater percentage of the community. And though this fragmented the congregation, they believed that reaching unchurched and dechurched people was a higher priority than maintaining internal cohesiveness. "After all," remarked Pastor Bill, "once you get over a hundred people, you don't know everybody anyway."

Corrective Step #2: Conduct multiple services at multiple times. This step requires looking at staffing, facility, and community needs.[11] Although it is never advisable to overwork volunteers, it is important to focus on the needs of your community along with the needs of your leaders.

Corrective Step #3: Conduct multiple services at multiple venues. Many churches are discovering the power of holding multiple services (either concurrently or at different times) at different venues or locations.[12] Often this "multiple venue strategy" uses live musicians to vary the worship style at each venue, but beams the speaker by live video or prerecorded DVD to all venues. Some churches do not even tell the congregants at which venue the speaker will appear live. An illustration of a church that is successfully using and expanding this multiple venue approach will be explored more fully later in this chapter.

Corrective Step #4: Build a new sanctuary with only 40 percent more capacity than your *largest current* celebration. Doing this will keep you from creating a worship space that is too cavernous and empty. An auditorium with too much space creates a feeling of desolation, which can sometimes create feelings of barrenness and even pessimism.

Corrective Step #5: Create unity among multiple services by hosting regular unity services. Four times a year, Mother's Day, midsummer or early fall, Thanksgiving, and Easter, host combined services to laud the congregation's unity in diversity. At these conclaves, combine the best musical groups, choirs, testimonies, and unique strengths from all your celebrations into one exciting package. The opportunity to celebrate many divergent styles, while embracing the same foundational theology, can be a powerful testimony to a watching world that is all too accustomed to schisms among Christians. And the size of a combined unity celebration often requires churches to hold these conclaves in civic auditoriums or schools. Again, this becomes a testimony to a watching world, when the true size of the congregation becomes evident.

Corrective Step #6: Be proactive in developing leaders for multiple worship services. A common error is to begin developing leaders for a new service once an existing service is nearing 80 percent capacity. If we grasp a mental picture that "the harvest is plentiful" (Luke 10:2), then we should be requesting "the Lord of the harvest, therefore, to send out workers into his harvest field" (Luke 10:2). To participate in this conscription, we should set up programs to train these leaders as the Lord provides them. Begin by identifying potential leaders and having them train alongside leaders during existing celebrations. Everyone should be mentoring an apprentice or trainee who may take over in his or her absence and/or as growth requires.

A SUCCESS STORY

First Christian Church of Canton, Ohio: Multiple Celebrations in Middle America

John Hampton is the teaching minister at First Christian Church of Canton, Ohio, and pastors a flock of more than two thousand people. But you wouldn't know it from the look of the sanctuary. It is long, narrow, and rather dark. The use of multiple worship services and venues allows First Christian Church to grow without having to rapidly expand facilities.

"It's part of our personality," stated John. "We live in a culture of choice, and as a true 'Multi-gen. Church,' we are reaching different generations with different worship options. This is our personality or, as some say, our philosophy of ministry." Figure 2.3 represents an overview of the current worship offerings along with conceptual ideas for future expansion.

Figure 2.3 Weekly Worship Options at First Christian Church, Canton, Ohio. Conceptual ideas for future services are outlined.

CURRENT WORSHIP OPTIONS, 1 TO 4	FUTURE WORSHIP OPTIONS, 1-A TO 4-B
CURRENT ATTENDANCE: 1,590–1,840	POTENTIAL ATTENDANCE: 4,700 + USING CURRENT FACILITIES
Celebration 1: SUNDAY 9:00 A.M. • Style: Traditional. • Target: Builder and Senior Generations, b. 1945 and before. • Size: 500–600 people. • Venue: main sanctuary with seating for 1,100.	**Celebration 1-A:** SUNDAY 9:00 A.M. • Style, target, and venue same as Celebration 1. **Celebration 1-B:** SUNDAY 9:00 A.M. • Same style and target as Celebration 1. • Different *venue,* in the chapel with seating for 300.
Celebration 2: SUNDAY 10:30 A.M. • Style: Modern. • Target: Boomer Generation, b. 1946–1964. • Size: 800–900 people. • Venue: main sanctuary with seating for 1,100.	**Celebration 2-A:** SUNDAY 10:30 A.M. • Style, target, and venue same as Celebration 2. **Celebration 2-B:** SUNDAY 10:30 A.M. • Same style and target as Celebration 2. • Different *venue,* in the chapel.
Celebration 3: SATURDAY 5:30 P.M. • Style: Modern. • Target: Boomer Generation, b. 1946–1964. • Size: 250–300. • Venue: chapel with seating for 300.	**Celebration 3-A:** SUNDAY 12 NOON • Same style, target, and *venue* as Celebration 3 (move to the sanctuary when needed). **Celebration 3-B:** SATURDAY 5:30 P.M. • Same style, target, and *venue* as Celebration 3 (move to the sanctuary when needed).
Celebration 4: TUESDAY 7:00 P.M. • Style: Postmodern. • Target: Gen X and Gen Y, b. 1965 and before. • Size: 100–140 people. • Venue: chapel with seating for 300.	**Celebration 4-A:** TUESDAY 7:00 P.M. • Same style, target, and *venue* as Celebration 4. **Celebration 4-B:** TUESDAY 7:00 P.M. • Same style and target as Celebration 4. • Different *venue,* in the sanctuary seating 1,100 or elsewhere.

"And I think it's important to have the same vision being cast at all services," continued John. "Rick Warren says the pulpit is like the rudder of the boat, a small part but with a great effect. If you want to have a common vision, you have to have a consistent voice."

I asked whether the people have become comfortable with the sermon on monitors and large screens. "The only people who look right at me are the ones in the first few pews," replied John. "Everyone, even the older people, watch the monitors. It's our culture; we're used to getting our information and education from TV and computer screens. Plus, people like it at church because they can see your expressions."

John summarized, "Though we're in the process of relocating and building a new sanctuary, we still plan on keeping multiple services and venues . . . we'll just have more room to grow. Our congregation doesn't expect to build one big room because people are going to choose to come to church when it's most convenient for them, not when it's most convenient for the church."

QUESTIONS FOR GROUP STUDY

The following questions are for group study:

1. How full are each of your services? Have you reached 80 percent of your *comfortable* capacity in any service? If so, what should you do about this? (See the suggestions in this chapter.)

2. Are you considering combining services? If so, who is driving this suggestion? Remember, a church's leaders will often inadvertently stress their felt needs over those of average attendees. Administer a questionnaire to discover your congregants' preferences for worship times and styles. Then factor in leaders' preferences, but give them no more influence than that of the average congregant.

3. Do you have multiple venues, either in your church or locally, that could be utilized for multiple venue worship? Make a list of all locations that could be suitable. Then rank them by suitability. Take the top three, and brainstorm the number of volunteers needed to staff each sufficiently. Now factor in the number of volunteers along with the suitability of each location to determine your top venue. Create action steps (with due dates attached) to launch a new venue worship when attendance allows.

4. If you have multiple services, when was the last time you had a combined unity service? If you have not hosted one in the past quarter, what obstacles must you overcome? What would be the benefits? Create an action plan with due dates to hold unity services.

CHAPTER 3

Missteps with Prayer

As one studies case histories of growing churches, there is one reoccurring factor—they are all praying *churches.*
                    —Eddie Gibbs, church growth scholar and researcher[1]

Factors That Cause Initial Growth in Churches	Erroneous Decisions That Lead to Plateauing	Corrective Steps to Regain Initial Growth
Urgency in prayer is due to potential for failure. Also, a significant portion of the prayer focus is on the unchurched and dechurched. (*Dechurched* is defined as "those who have terminated their attendance elsewhere due to some real or perceived hurt, conflict, etc.")	Security in circumstances robs prayer of its urgency. Prayer focus is also increasingly on the needs of church attendees rather than on dechurched and unchurched people. In addition, institutionalization of prayer takes place. Prayer forms are standardized and formalized, especially in the church celebration.	Don't wait for a crisis to reinvigorate the prayer life of a church. Consider the enormity and significance of the task you are undertaking: the Great Commission (Matt. 28:18-20). Also, employ 50/50 prayer, where 50% of the prayer focus is on congregational needs while the other 50% addresses the needs of the unchurched and dechurched.

From Powerhouse to Poorhouse

"This is a beautiful prayer room. But notice how far it is from the new sanctuary. That sort of represents how our focus on prayer has shifted."

"This used to be the 'powerhouse' of the church," began Everett, the pastor of Plymouth Church. As I looked down an elongated and musty-smelling room beneath the church's former sanctuary, I noticed it was filled with odd pieces of furniture and broken chairs. "You wouldn't believe the prayer-power that was released here," continued Everett. "Some people have called the prayer room the powerhouse of a church, and this was certainly the powerhouse for us."

A few hours and a few miles later, we were headed out of Plymouth's new sanctuary and down a corridor to another prayer room, this one markedly brighter, cleaner, and better smelling. "This is a beautiful prayer room," said Everett. "But notice how far it is from the new sanctuary. That sort of represents how our focus on prayer has shifted."

Within fifteen years Plymouth had grown from a dying church into a large, but plateaued congregation of nine hundred weekend attendees. The journey from the first facility on Plymouth Street had taken three steps, first to a nearby community movie theater, then to an empty supermarket, and now to a beautiful new facility.

"Theaters don't usually have space for prayer rooms," remembered Everett. "So we lowered a curtain in the middle of the stage and made a prayer room right behind the pulpit area. I guess it was about twelve feet by thirty feet, and it was probably even in a better location than the prayer room under the old sanctuary. It helped keep our focus on prayer because it was central to our auditorium. Eventually, we needed four services to accommodate an attendance of almost thirteen hundred.

"Our third facility was not nearly as convenient for prayer. It was a former supermarket, and the best location for a prayer room was a small office near the front. But that seemed okay because a lot of other ministries were jockeying for space.

However, our prayer emphasis changed to navel-gazing. We prayed more about the needs of our church members than of those who didn't come to church. Now we're in a new facility. And the prayer room is gorgeous, but it's not used much."

"Why the drop-off in participation?" I asked.

"It seems there are several reasons," continued Everett. "First, we don't emphasize prayer and reaching the lost the way we used to. Second, the prayer gathering doesn't feel like a powerhouse anymore. We're a lot more subdued and reflective. And finally, I think the prayer room is too disconnected from the sanctuary. It's down this long hallway, and few people can find it. I guess the best location was near the pulpit area. As the prayer room moved farther from the sanctuary, I think it reflected how prayer became less central to our church."

Factors That Caused Initial Growth

The following factors came to light during interviews at Plymouth Church:

Cause of Growth #1: There was an urgency in prayer due to a potential for failure. Fifteen years earlier, the congregation had been a dying church on Plymouth Street. When Everett arrived, he felt overwhelmed with the task, and that drove him to prayer. Soon Everett implemented a comprehensive prayer ministry, which attracted many congregants with similar concerns. Soon, that musty storage room below the sanctuary had become a clean, pleasant, and well-attended powerhouse of prayer.

Cause of Growth #2: There was broad participation in prayer. Before Everett arrived, Plymouth had few active ministries. As a result, when Everett suggested a prayer focus, a sizable church constituency readily embraced it.

Cause of Growth #3: Prayer was supernatural, dynamic, and spontaneous. The vibrancy of the church's prayer life led to an abundance of supernatural encounters. And as the church began to grow, the sense of divine presence and intervention further increased the centrality and excitement about prayer. Even in the worship services, spontaneity and expectancy accompanied prayer.

Cause of Growth #4: The focus on prayer resulted in close attention to the results of prayer. Because prayer was central to the church's personality, there was a corresponding attention to results. A large bulletin board was covered with note cards listing specific prayer requests, each leaving space to add the eventual answer to that prayer. This attention to results helped build reliance on and certainty in God's responses to prayer.

Cause of Growth #5: The prayer room was closely linked to the worship area. In Everett's mind, the proximity of the prayer room to the sanctuary reflected the congregation's mental link between prayer and worship. As the room inadvertently moved farther from the sanctuary, so did the centrality and visibility of prayer gradually ebb.

Cause of Growth #6: Prayer focused on reaching the unchurched and dechurched. To survive, the church needed to grow. And thus, it aggressively prayed for people in the area who needed a church home.

Cause of Growth #7: God responded to prayer. Since evangelism is a work of the Holy Spirit (John 16:8-9), and God promises to respond to vibrant and passionate prayers of virtuous people (2 Chron. 7:14; James 5:16), the church's prayer focus unleashed growth.

Erroneous Decisions That Led to Plateauing

The following erroneous decisions slowly, but deliberately, contributed to a halt in growth:

Error 1: Urgency and emphasis on prayer faded. The divergent and pressing concerns of a growing church pushed aside the more tedious but critical emphasis on prayer. Urgency, due in part to the potential for failure, was replaced with a growing triviality toward prayer. Though prayer may be lauded and emphasized, it sometimes cannot compete with more ostentatious endeavors.

Error 2: Those with the "gift" of intercessory prayer were delegated the responsibility to pray, exempting those with the "role" of prayer. In his book on spiritual gifts, Peter Wagner stresses that though God has "gifted" certain individuals with extraordinary proficiency in intercessory prayer, everyone has the responsibility, duty, or "role" to engage in prayer.[2] In the prayer meetings at Plymouth those leaders without the gift of intercessory prayer began to delegate to "gifted" intercessors the task of prayer. Though most of the leaders still had the "role" of prayer, prayer seemed less urgent, and the leaders impulsively delegated their responsibility. As a result, there was not universal participation in prayer as there once was and should be.

Error 3: The sense of the supernatural was replaced with a sense of formalization and standardization. The sense of supernatural intervention and spontaneity was slowly replaced with a sense of institutionalism as prayer forms were standardized and formalized. "Prayer became focused more on ceremony than survival," recalled Everett. Supernatural encounters were less expected and, as a result, less encountered.

Error 4: Tracking the results of prayer became less common. The church's survival no longer seemed so closely tied to specific answers to prayer. And this sense of stability and security robbed prayer not only of its urgency, but also of the need to carefully track the answers to prayer.

Error 5: Prayer became disconnected from the worship venue. The prayer room was moved to locations that were increasingly less visible to the congregation. And this subtly reflected the growing detachment of the prayer room from its centrality in the congregation.

Error 6: Prayer emphasis was increasingly on the needs of the congregation rather than on the unchurched and dechurched. As we saw in chapter 1, the needs of a growing congregation can often take precedence over the needs of the churched and unchurched. At Plymouth, a greater percentage of prayer became focused on the churched.

Error 7: The link between prayer and evangelism was gradually ignored. As we saw in the causes for growth, God responds to vibrant and passionate prayers of virtuous people. A waning corporate emphasis on this appears to have resulted in fewer responses on God's behalf.

Corrective Steps to Regain Growth

Nine Corrective Steps for Maintaining Vibrancy and Centrality in Prayer

Only the Holy Spirit can convict of wrongdoing, call to repentance, and lead to conversion (John 16:8-9). And thus, prayer becomes our priority. The following steps can help ensure that prayer retains the central focus and vibrancy it requires:

Corrective Step #1: Understand that having a virtuous life and conduct is a prerequisite for answered prayer. As James reminds us, "The prayer of a righteous man is powerful and effective" (James 5:16). And 2 Chronicles 7:14 stresses the corporate nature of this, as God declares, "If my people, who are called by my name, will humble themselves and pray and seek my face and turn from their wicked ways, then will I hear from heaven." Thus, any plan that seeks to create an effective prayer strategy must begin with discipleship and modeling of personal and corporate righteousness.

Corrective Step #2: Encourage senior vision-setting leaders to actively participate in prayer opportunities. Many leaders are endowed with administrative, leadership, pastoral, prophetic, teaching, and other such spiritual gifts (Rom. 12:6-8; 1 Cor. 12:7-11, 28; Eph. 4:11; 1 Pet. 4:9-10). Since many of these leaders do not possess the "gift of intercessory prayer," but only the duty or "role" of prayer, they can be tempted to delegate prayer to those with the "gift." If the leader is a vision caster, then he or she may need to be more involved in prayer than he or she feels is necessary because churches often reflect the personalities of their vision casters. For example, an athletic pastor may find the church he or she leads has an unusually large number of sport teams and/or ministries. Thus, because the church subtly takes on the personality of the pastor and prayer is so important, the pastor must be actively involved in the prayer opportunities of the church.

Corrective Step #3: Create prayer spaces. Terry Teykl, a United Methodist pastor, tells the remarkable story of how the church he pastored and others like it have experienced extraordinary growth rates once permanent "prayer rooms" were established. These are spaces designated for prayer, stocked with inspirational and informative prayer tools such as maps of the area, lists of community, state, and national leaders, along with compilations of the prayer needs of the congregation and community. Teykl's book, *Making Room to Pray*, is an effective guide for creating a functional and central prayer room ministry.[3]

Corrective Step #4: Create prayer networks. Here are three effective prayer strategies that can connect people into prayer networks:

- *Prayer Triplets* link three people to pray on a regular basis for needs of the church as well as for needs of unchurched and dechurched people. Prayer Triplets can be convened over the phone, over a cup of coffee, during a lunch break, or over the Internet. The Billy Graham Evangelistic Association uses Prayer Triplets extensively.

- *Community Prayer Networks* (CPNs) link people in geographical proximity to pray for neighborhood residents. These networks regularly communicate in a fashion similar to Prayer Triplets, that is, through the Internet, over the phone, in person. CPNs are larger groups, sometimes reaching a dozen or more people. A type of localized and neighborhood-based small group, they often meet face-to-face once or more a month.

- *Prayer Chains* are perhaps the oldest, and still one of the most effective, avenues for creating prayer networks. Based on the concept of a calling circle or chain, the "telephone effect" of exaggeration can be a concern. This can be reduced by utilizing chains conducted over the Internet where forwarding a written request thwarts embellishment errors.

Corrective Step #5: Keep prayer spaces in close proximity to the worship venue. As we saw at Plymouth Church, prayer's centrality can wane as prayer venues become less noticeable or less centrally located. Give the prayer room and ministry a visibility and accessibility reflecting its centrality in your church.

Corrective Step #6: Track prayer results. Chronicling the answers to prayers is done not to verify the presence of the supernatural, but to celebrate God's interaction. And thus, tracking prayer results should never be simply narcissistic calculus. Rather, answers to prayer can be tracked, as Jesus did when the seventy-two disciples returned from their ministry journey (Luke 10:1-23), as a way of observing and celebrating the Holy Spirit's workings.

Corrective Step #7: Consider a staff-level position for prayer intercessor. Some congregations have discovered the effectiveness of hiring a full-time intercessor on behalf of the congregation and its mission. Though care must be taken that this does not excuse those with the "role" of prayer from executing their duty, Peter Wagner muses that he finds it "curious that churches have not added staff members to give themselves to intercession—other staff is employed for just about everything else."[4]

Corrective Step #8: Utilize 50/50 prayer.[5] In this strategy 50/50 describes prayer that is equally balanced between prayer for church attendees and prayer for those who are unchurched or dechurched. As churches grow, an increasing percentage of congregational prayer tends to be focused toward the needs of current attendees. As a result, prayer for those outside the church is often overlooked and/or demoted. A 50/50 prayer focus does not mean spending less time praying for the needs of attendees, but extending prayer time to allow half of your emphasis to be focused toward the unchurched and dechurched.

Corrective Step #9: Make 50/50 prayer a part of every prayer opportunity. Whether a prayer from the pulpit or a prayer before a church dinner, utilizing 50/50 prayer helps keep the focus of the church on both the needs of the saints and the needs of the unchurched/dechurched.

A SUCCESS STORY

Mount Horeb United Methodist Church, Lexington, South Carolina: A Prayer-Driven Story

"When I got here, there were eighty-four in worship," began Pastor Jeff Kersey. "Now, nine years later we're about one thousand. People ask us what's the key. I tell them it's because we're a prayer-driven church.

"It all began when I started a 6:45 A.M. Friday prayer breakfast for men. But we structured it differently. Our primary focus was not on congregational needs. Instead, we spent most of our time praying and focusing on the unchurched.

"Then we walked through our church asking God to fill the pews with needy people. And people started showing up! So we dedicated Monday to prayer and fasting. But you are exactly on target about how you can forget those things that started growth. Eventually, fasting and prayer faded out on Monday. But now we know that was a mistake and have reinstituted it.

"Soon we were rapidly growing, and everybody knew prayer was driving the growth. So we called ourselves a 'prayer-driven' church. That's even on our church sign.

"Plus, part of our stewardship commitment every fall is to ask everyone to commit to a certain number of minutes each week to pray for the unchurched. And we're challenging each member to share Christ with three people this year. Right now we dedicate 46,000 prayer minutes each week to this outreach!

"We are also working a layperson into a full-time prayer coordinator. We have a lot of prayer ministries to oversee. We have a Tuesday morning prayer breakfast for teenagers that's structured like the Friday one, but it's better attended, even by teenagers at 6:45 A.M.! We have a prayer chapel where people sign up to pray. And we do a yearly prayer conference to mentor other churches.

"One thing that amazes me is how guests react so positively to prayer at the altar during worship services. We have thirty to seventy people who come forward to pray. And I get feedback all the time saying, 'It's great. I've never seen people go forward in prayer before.'

51

"Finally, community prayer boxes are really effective.[6] People volunteer to take a prayer box to a local business. It has a pad of paper attached and people are invited to put their prayer requests in the box. Then the volunteer regularly picks up the requests, and we pray for them in our prayer room. And if they leave contact information, we give them a phone call or mail them a note, letting them know they've been prayed for.

"Prayer is the key catalyst for change in any church," summarized Jeff. "It releases the Holy Spirit to lead a church into the congregation God meant it to be. From my experience, I'd say you can't change without starting with a 'prayer-driven church.'"

QUESTIONS FOR GROUP STUDY

The following questions are for group study:

1. Do you recall a time when the church was growing and healthy? What was the role of prayer at that time? Did it have the same centrality and vivacity as it has today? If not, list specific changes. Are there strategies in this chapter that you could use to reestablish prayer's centrality? List them by suitability, and make an action plan to begin with your top two choices.

2. Is prayer a central part of your church's personality? Ask guests and newcomers by a simple and anonymous questionnaire to rank the top five positive characteristics of your church. If prayer is not listed among the five, should it be? And if it should, what will you do to become a prayer-driven church? Launch an action plan to make prayer more central to your congregation.

3. Have your leaders taken a "spiritual gifts inventory" in the last eighteen months?

- If you answered yes, how many people in your congregation have the gift of intercessory prayer? And how many are actively involved in prayer ministries? Based on the ideas presented in this chapter, what should you do?
- If you answered no, would taking a spiritual gifts inventory be helpful? If so, contact your local Christian bookstore to secure copies.

4. What does it mean that all Christians have the "role" of prayer? And what does the author mean by writing that vision-casting leaders may need to be more involved in prayer than they feel is necessary? Is this true in your circumstance? If it is, what should be done?

5. How widespread is involvement in your prayer ministries? Tally the percentage of members who are engaged in or attend prayer opportunities in your church. If the figure is below 40 percent, there may be cause for concern. What strategies could you employ to increase participation in prayer opportunities?

6. How much of your prayers are directed toward the unchurched? Do you practice 50/50 prayer? Do you practice this universally? Begin to employ 50/50 prayer in every prayer opportunity. Then, once a month, evaluate your results.

CHAPTER 4

Missteps with Budgets

In the house of the wise are stores of choice food and oil,
but a foolish man devours all he has.

—Proverbs 21:20

Factors That Cause Initial Growth in Churches	Erroneous Decisions That Lead to Plateauing	Corrective Steps to Regain Initial Growth
Budget is structured and conservative, primarily based on money in hand.	Budgeting is overly optimistic, based upon the euphoria of initial growth. In the name of flexibility the structure of the budgeting process may also be scrapped. If growth slows, fiscal flexibility will tighten quickly and dramatically, often leading to conflict and tension.	Budget more conservatively and more intentionally than you feel you should. Church leaders are often optimists, but basing budgets on overly optimistic projections or eschewing budget procedures in the name of flexibility can be reckless.

How Good Ideas Can Overpower Budgets

"When God opens the windows of heaven, it seems almost unspiritual to slow down and study what you're supposed to do next."

These were heady times. The church had started off as a medium-sized, traditional congregation, but in less than four years had passed the one thousand mark in attendance. The church had successfully unified its newcomers and longtime members.[1] In addition, many newcomers brought with them innovative ideas on how to reach out to their friends.

The church hired a certified public accountant to help keep track of its expanding budget. Jim had attended the church for years and blended in nicely with the staff. "I knew I wanted a numbers guy," confided the senior pastor. "He helped us keep our heads on straight and our budgets in line." With Jim's assistance, burgeoning ministries established realistic budgets and fiscal guidelines.

Another reason for budgetary conservatism was the memory, fresh in the leaders' minds, of being a plateaued church only four years before. But soon with growth taking place, they began to throw open the doors to more aggressive financial forecasts and proposals. Jim's rising protestations were considered, but often clandestinely cast aside in favor of ministry expansion. In fact, there was a growing opinion that budgetary regulations and procedures were becoming cumbersome, perhaps even unspiritual. "When God opens the windows of heaven," the senior pastor observed later, "it seems almost unspiritual to slow down and study what you're supposed to do next."

A weekly planning meeting sprang from this surplus in funds. It was designed to delve into the ministry proposals the church leaders received each week and to select the best for implementation. Everyone relished this enclave, for here young men and women explained new ideas for ministry. If a program showed promise, before long it was launched and new people were hired (if even just part-time initially). Although the staff conducted three worship services every weekend, one pastor confessed that he often sensed the Holy Spirit's presence more strongly at this meeting than at any other time during the week.

The Difference Five Years Can Make

Five years later, I was walking down a different hall, but headed to the same meeting I just described. This time, however, my pace was markedly slower. As I turned the corner toward the conference room, I noticed the door was uncharacteristically shut. Nevertheless, the volume of the discussion was not being contained within the walls.

Within a few minutes the door abruptly opened and a staff member I knew as Barry hurried by. Without speaking a word he exited, not toward the office wing, but down the stairs and out of the building.

Over the next two hours we discussed the reasons behind Barry's departure. Barry (a pseudonym) had been the church's director of counseling. Due to rising budgetary problems, Barry had been asked to cut back to part-time status with the counseling department, filling the rest of his day with janitorial duties. Years before as a college student, Barry had been on the custodial crew of the church, but after one of those high-spirited planning sessions, he had been tapped to oversee the church's new counseling ministry. Barry had worked quite happily as both counselor and custodian in his early years. Now, having earned his degree in psychology, he greatly relished this counseling ministry, developing it into a network of lay counselors.

However, money had become tight. Gradually, the euphoria of growth had led to an overprojection of budgets. Jim, a regular remonstrator against such overprojection, felt increasingly that his admonitions were not being considered. And thus, only a year before, Jim had resigned. His position was filled by a well-meaning, talented man with a background in starting up new businesses. But the new administrator was more skilled in entrepreneurship than fiscal supervision; he allowed new ideas to be implemented with overly aggressive budgets. Soon, the church was living well beyond its means. Belt-tightening and sacrifices were required. Some church leaders, noting that Barry had once happily balanced both janitorial and counseling duties, felt he should be willing to do so again.

Barry's departure that day did not arise from the lack of a servant's heart. Rather, his frustration had been fueled by a growing impression that monetary concerns were misdirecting the church's focus away from compassion. And Barry, like most of the church's leaders, was unsure how to return to those days when ministry and money flowed unabated. In confusion, frustration, and desperation, Barry left—both the meeting and the church.

"We were a lot more careful with budgets early on," recalled the senior pastor. "But when growth that big happens, you forget the discipline that got you there."

Barry soon entered law school and at last report was a successful and empathetic legal advocate. Barry's gifts had opened doors for him at one time in the church's history, but toward the end, fiscal missteps had closed that path.

How Optimism Can Overpower Budgets

"When a man stepped forward with a $17,000 gift, there was a real feeling that it saved our hides."

The second example comes from a young church planter, who at his denomination's request planted churches in Indiana and Illinois. Only age twenty-four at the onset, he sensed the heavy responsibility that was thrust upon him. "But I felt somewhat up to the task because as a layperson in my school years, I had been involved in three other church plants," David recalled. He launched into the endeavor with gusto and zeal. In fact, his enthusiasm led to his selection as the founding pastor of this newly planted church. But his zeal and optimism soon got the better of his budgetary strategies.

"The first year I was pretty cautious with our budget," David said. "You don't make aggressive plans for budgets when you are inexperienced. I guess inexperience can be a good counterbalance for enthusiasm."

But as the church started to grow, David's insecurity waned. "We started to grow, and I planned for a second year's budget that included a great deal of faith," stated David. "In our denomination we create a budget and have it approved by the district board. . . . The problem was, they gave me more control than I probably should have received. The budget I came up with was largely speculative and overly optimistic. I thought we'd be 150 [in attendance] by the end of the year. But when that didn't pan out, we were in trouble. We didn't hit our growth projections, and we didn't hit our budget either. When a man stepped forward with an unexpected $17,000 gift, there was a real feeling that it saved our hides.

"A final mistake was not taking enough time to plan the budget." David summarized: "I was required by the district to prepare a June-to-May budget. Prior to our launch, I spent a lot of time working on the budget. But by year two I was working on the budget around May 15 for a June 1 deadline. In that amount of time you just don't have time to look at the past or what other churches are doing. Year two certainly wasn't budget realism. It was guesswork. But I was zealous to move ahead, no matter what."

David's situation was too similar to that of many pastors sent to plant churches or bring change to aging congregations. While denominational leaders walk a fine line between being micromanagers and giving creative leaders too much leeway in budgeting, too often the budget is not watched sufficiently. The result can be unrealistic projections by the pastors. Their enthusiasm, vision, and faith—the very gifts that make them ideal for the planting or change process—can also be weak spots in their planning strategies.

When planting a church or helping a church undertake needed changes, a congregation can too quickly outpace meager funds and end up in a financial mess. "Church planter and change advocate types tend to be better with people than paper. That's our problem," mused David in hindsight.

Solomon Understood Budgetary Dangers

Both congregations are similar to the foolhardy man about whom Solomon lamented. Well acquainted with exhilarating years of luxury and abundance, Solomon reflected that "in the house of the wise are stores of choice food and oil, but a foolish man devours all he has" (Prov. 21:20).

Solomon had come of age during the heady years of his father David's kingdom, but upon his ascension to the throne, Solomon probably inherited a stagnated economy accompanied by growing hostilities with neighboring nations. When penning this proverb, Solomon might have been recalling the story of Joseph (Gen. 37–50) and how he had commended himself to Pharaoh by suggesting that Egypt store up food during years of abundance to compensate for an impending famine. Or perhaps Solomon was just reflecting on wise economic acumen that he received from God and/or experience.

Either way, many theologians and archaeologists are convinced that Solomon employed strict fiscal oversights to keep ancient Israel fiscally viable, at least until the rivalries of David's other offspring tore Israel apart. But the lesson here is that wise fiscal planning should include at least some element of storing up resources (the "choice food and oil" of Solomon's analogy) while being cautious not to "devour all one has" and be left without reserves for unforeseen slowdowns, problems, and/or plateaus.

Factors That Caused Initial Growth

What were the contributing forces that inaugurated growth in both congregations, one an older congregation, and the other a newly started congregation?

Cause of Growth #1: Initially, both congregations budgeted conservatively, based upon money they had in hand. They looked closely at last year's budget or denominational recommendations and were careful not to exceed it. They did not overestimate their budgets and have to request cutbacks and resignations.

But as growth began, even meagerly, it outpaced their fairly cautious projections. In that environment the staff, though often busy, worked happily as unforeseen financial surpluses opened up new opportunities. A spirit of toil, but also expectation, imbued both congregations.

Thus, at first both churches budgeted sensibly and conserva-tively, yet still inaugurated new ideas and directions. And new ministries had a chance to succeed without pressure to quickly "add numbers" to the church's attendance. Granted, viable min-istries should eventually be fiscally sound, but that usually does not occur until a time of development and fine-tuning takes place. Conservative budgetary practices, early in a church's career or turnaround, can give ministries time to develop and be modified without undue pressure to contribute to the financial base.

Conservative budgeting occurred, not because of any grand design, but because the situation demanded it. Initially, both con-gregations' fiscal outlook was tempered by the low or slow growth they experienced at the beginning of life and renewal, respectively. In other words, the church leaders budgeted conser-vatively because they had only meager funds with which to work.

Cause of Growth #2: Both congregations had employed structured budgetary policies. They applied deadlines and appraisals to each item within their budget. Doing this forced the congregations to think deliberately about each fiscal outlay, con-sidering the ramifications and benefits of each. Establishing budgets, evaluating them at year's end, and developing a budget for the following year taught deliberateness and organization.

However, as growth began to increase in both congregations, a euphoric atmosphere of change took hold. Budgetary constraints seemed cumbersome, perhaps even unspiritual. That led to the following erroneous decisions that soon plateaued growth.

Erroneous Decisions That Led to Plateauing

Most pastors and denominational leaders have stories similar to one of the examples discussed here. The overprojection of fiscal viability and the setting aside of vital (but sometimes cumbersome) budgetary procedures seem to be common, but all too deadly, occurrences. And so, the churches in our examples suddenly found themselves in a quandary that many churches experience.

Such fiscal missteps do not assail every church, and some avoid the pitfalls. But it has been my observation that a majority of growing churches eventually succumb to this malady. They embrace a financial model that is influenced by euphoric periods of growth and budgetary surplus. Earlier in the process the same churches may have been fiscally conservative because of the uncertainty of newness or because their plateaued status necessitated it. When growth occurs, optimism rises also. As a result, risky financial missteps too often follow.

This scenario is created in part because the realm of financial projections is an often bewildering field. Regrettably, pastors do not receive in seminary or college adequate training in these important disciplines. Yet no business school graduate would be allowed to matriculate without at least two courses in financial budgeting and planning.

Unsure how to handle burgeoning growth and the cryptic realm of financial forecasting, both churches made two key missteps.

Error 1: The churches overprojected future income. The euphoria associated with a burgeoning congregation, along with the rapidly increasing income that accompanied it, caused the church leaders to overproject future income. They allowed the excitement generated by the inauguration of growth to cause them to overestimate their financial prowess. And as a result of the cutbacks, tensions, and bickering that followed, growth prematurely halted, and a decline ensued.

Error 2: They set aside budgetary procedures and evaluations. As we saw in the illustrations, circumventing the planning process, even in the name of flexibility, can be unwise and sometimes inaugurate resource-consuming programs. With extra monies available for new projects, there often develops an unspoken adage that new programs can be funded without too much forward thinking or ongoing appraisal. Rather than going through a budgetary review process that may take time, leaders short-circuit the procedure because funds are at the ready. Eventually, this fiscal flexibility becomes established as an unspoken, but accepted policy. Soon, entire segments of the church's ministry may be funded outside a planned and structured budgeting process.

When a church experiences a plateau or slowdown in growth, it is ill prepared for what lies ahead. Again, the usual results are confusion, discord, and dissent. Since staff salaries often make up a sizable portion of the budget (and facilities are less easy to shed than staff), employees are encouraged to resign or retire, but if need be, they will be fired.

Too often in the church, because of overly optimistic projections or lack of discipline, we forge ahead into a gloomy future of overdue bills, staff exits, and downsizing.

Corrective Steps to Regain Growth

Budget More Conservatively and Intentionally Than You Think You Can or Should

As Christians, we are an optimistic lot. And why shouldn't we be? Faith is a touchstone of our belief. The author of Hebrews gave us a definitive description of it, stating, "Now faith is being sure of what we hope for and certain of what we do not see. This is what the ancients were commended for" (Heb. 11:1-2).

Sometimes as Christian leaders, we can feel that our faith in things "hoped for" may result in "commendation" from both God and humankind. But when hope mutates into presumption, and throwing off restraints leads us to embrace unrealistic conjecture, we run the risk of damaging the church's viability and credibility.

Corrective Step #1: Budget in a more conservative, structured, and organized manner than you might think you should or can. Often in organizations starting to grow there is a desire to inculcate so much flexibility that budgeting happens on the fly. Pastors and parishioners come up with good ideas that need "immediate implementation." The excitement of growth drives the engine and often clouds the judgment. And one successful program gives credence to another. Often I have witnessed programs that seemed to spring from the flotsam and jetsam of another successful endeavor. Often these secondary off-spring do not have the thought, planning, and foresight of their progenitors. As such, they may launch the church into directions that are not appropriate or productive.

In his seminal book on why certain businesses make the leap from "good to great," Jim Collins states that "good-to-great companies built a consistent system with clear constraints, but they also gave people freedom and responsibility within the framework of that system." [2] In other words, they established procedures, checks, and constraints but also allowed a great deal of creativity within that framework.

Budgeting conservatively and requiring structure in the budgeting process eliminate not all, but a significant portion of the problem. Such a strategy allows a program leader to think through the focus as well as the implementation of a program. Budgeting conservatively and early also forces creative individuals to take a moment and consider their plans. It forces discretion and discrimination upon the creative leaders whose minds (and ideas) work at twice the speed of more typical intellects.

Here then is the first corrective step: budget in a more conservative, structured, and organized manner than you feel you can or should. Do not let optimism, the inauguration of growth, or he perceived success of another program lure you into overly aggressive projections. Budget more conservatively and deliberately.

Corrective Step #2: Employ the 80-10-10 principle in church budgeting. A popular axiom among Christian financial advisors has been the 80-10-10 principle. Briefly stated, it suggests that a responsible Christian should manage one's finances in an 80-10-10 ratio. In this ratio, the 80 percent represents the portion of an individual's income on which one should live. The 10 percent represents the tithe, or tenth, of the income that is designated for charitable giving. The remaining percentage represents a 10 percent savings or investment of that income.

Such a practice accomplishes three things. First, it teaches the individual how to live in a reasonable and sound fiscal manner. Living on 80 percent of one's income may seem difficult after years of feasting on 100 percent, but once attained it gives a sense of security and self-sufficiency that living on the financial edge cannot match.

Second, this practice appropriately returns to God a tithe of the individual's income. Such charitable giving, though a concept with Old Testament roots (Mal. 3:6-12), appears to receive indirect validation from Jesus in Matthew 23:23. Regardless of whether this is a biblical mandate or inference, tithing 10 percent of each member's income allows the church to be fiscally viable and vibrant.

Third, the 80-10-10 principle promotes saving a 10 percent portion for future advantage. Polls and magazine articles continually lament that Americans are weak in the area of savings. Setting aside savings in a consumer-driven economy is sometimes difficult to keep in focus. However, financial experts warn us that living without financial savings can be irresponsible and dangerous. In addition, putting away a tenth of one's income, when invested appropriately, can quickly mushroom into a large fiscal reserve.

The 80-10-10 budgetary principle has much to commend it in the church context as well. In the church scenario, 80 percent would be designated for the church's operating budget. The next 10 percent would represent a tithe or charitable gift of its income. Many churches typically follow this last suggestion, investing a portion, though not always as high as 10 percent, in charitable, denominational, and/or missionary endeavors.

Yet a growing number of churches are finding the wisdom and sensibility of designating 10 percent of their income for savings. This burgeoning nest egg gives the church a sense of fiscal strength and durability. The mental tranquillity alone may be worth the effort.

Churches handle this growing reserve in different ways. The most popular is not to touch the savings until a crisis arises; thus, a new roof or boiler might be funded from this reserve.

Other churches are discovering the prudence of holding the entire amount in savings and using only the interest for expenditures. Initially, before the fund has grown to significant size, it may be a trivial sum, so many churches initially opt not to pursue this route. However, this route may be even more difficult to pursue once a church has become accustomed to dipping into this fund whenever a perceived emergency arrives.

The best process, if feasible, is to invest 10 percent of a church's income and spend only the return on the investment. By setting aside this 10 percent on a monthly basis, a church may see its nest egg soon accrue into a sizable sum. Subsequently, the church may spend the return on this investment on a regular basis to fund needed updates, repairs, and innovative ministries. Granted, sometimes pressing financial needs may occur that require dipping into this fund for the sake of preserving the church and/or its facility. But this should be the exception to the rule, undertaken only after careful appraisal of the church's predicament and the repercussions of the action.

A SUCCESS STORY

Springlake Wesleyan Church, Springlake, Michigan:
From Overbudgeting to Realistic Budgeting

"I really learned a lot coming here. Planting a church was
a learning experience, but in many ways coming to an
established church helped me learn many things, like
budgeting, the right way."

A strong dose of pragmatism was thrust upon this twenty-year-old "Connections Pastor" when he moved from the church he planted to become staff pastor at a rapidly growing church in western Michigan. Before accepting his position as the pastor responsible for "connecting" newcomers and parishioners within this large church, he had been a church planter in nearby Indiana and Illinois. "I really learned a lot coming here," he stated. "Planting a church was a learning experience, but in many ways coming to an established church helped me learn many things, like budgeting, the right way," recollected David.

Yes, David was the church planter of the earlier example in this chapter. Now, he finds himself as an associate pastor at a large church in Spring Lake, Michigan.

Spring Lake Wesleyan Church, thanks in part to an emphasis on realistic budgeting, is not only growing but is also enjoying new options and opportunities in ministry. From our conversations came two examples of how budgeting conservatively and deliberately can alleviate stress and increase ministry.

It helps to set up your budgets early and review them regularly.

"Here [at Spring Lake Wesleyan] we have to budget early," David began. "This allows programs time to be examined and structured before we try them. It used to be that when I came up with an idea, I wanted to get it done in a month. Now we must set our budgets by the end of January for a budget beginning June 1. It forces me to review each program to make the best use of the resources I'm allocated. And if I have a new idea, I have to wait and launch it in due time. One lesson I'm learning here is that church planters and turnaround leaders could do better if they didn't give up on early planning and ongoing review. I guess it's because people like me are sometimes visionary to a fault."

Few would deny that David's vision and faith-filled outlook were assets in his ministry, but the fiscal parameters put upon him corralled that energy and matured him into an effective and far more strategic planner.

Don't plan on benefactors to rescue overly optimistic budgets.

David also learned that leaders shouldn't count on unforeseen gifts to rescue their budgets. "Unexpected gifts give us flexibility at Spring Lake," mused David. "Here they give us opportunities rather than just keeping us afloat. In the church plants I was in before, there was a feeling that unexpected gifts were needed to bail us out. And when they came in, there was a big sigh of relief.

"But now when unexpected money comes in, it is an incredible opportunity instead of a bandage. When it happens here, we begin to dream about how we can increase ministry. It's a great feeling! Budgeting realism is a more exciting way to live than on the budgetary edge. And preparation and planning can help you keep your focus on people as individuals with needs rather than givers who can save your hide."

Figure 4.1 How budgets were set in David's two church experiences.

David's experience in the second year of church plants	David's experience at Spring Lake Church
MAY 1 Start thinking about the budget, due June 1.	JANUARY 1-31 Write budgets within each department and submit to the oversight committee.
MAY 15 Hastily send a budget to the oversight committee. There is no time to study past history or program appropriateness.	FEBRUARY 1–MAY 31 Study and analyze budgets. Fine-tune budgets in cooperation with the oversight committee and individual departments.
JUNE 1–MAY 31 Don't worry about budgets until crises arrive. Depend upon unexpected gifts to "save your hide."	JUNE 1–MAY 31 Use budgets, monitoring monthly. Allow unexpected gifts to foster innovation and flexibility.
Which David are you?	

Don't Forget: Your Budget Is a Plan—and a Prediction!

A final word about budgets is in order. Budgets are often misunderstood as only a means for control. But thinking of budgets only in this light limits their potential. In actuality, budgets forecast what an organization does, how it does it, when it does it, and how long it does it. As a result, a budget is not just a method for control; it is also an integral tool for mapping out the future.

Noted management scholar Aaron Wildavsky emphasizes in *The New Politics of the Budgetary Process* that "a budget is really a prediction."[3] By this, he means that a budget establishes and supports "intended behavior" and thus is a "prediction" of what is intended to take place.[4] As such, it is important that visionaries have significant input into a budget's creation to ensure the budget fiscally supports the predictions the church has made about its future ministry.

But Wildavsky states that "a budget is also a plan,"[5] and plans must be realistic, obtainable, and not recklessly optimistic. Thus, those setting the budget must include individuals whose careful attention to detail and analysis can ensure the church does not budget too aggressively or too modestly for realistic growth.

Corrective Step #3: Make sure your budget process includes visionary people along with individuals gifted in attentiveness to detail and assessment. In your budget planning process solicit participation from visionary/creative people and individuals gifted in attentiveness to facts and evaluation. Keep in mind that both perspectives are needed in the budgetary process and are not mutually exclusive.

In addition, be sure that forward thinkers as well as pragmatics have equal access to ongoing budgetary review. Management researcher Fred David believes that regularly evaluating budgetary items by creative thinkers along with more analytical thinkers is the best way to make "profitable use of an organization's resources (i.e., people)."[6]

While having reasonable and fitting budgetary projections is important, they nonetheless must be visionary. Any budget that does not help a church see the future and move toward it will stagnate that church, leading to a plateauing in growth—or worse.

QUESTIONS FOR GROUP STUDY

Permit each leader to answer the ten questions below privately on a piece of paper. Then join together and compare your observations. Devel further by asking the group these questions:

- In light of this chapter, what are our responses telling you about where our congregation is headed?
- And in light of this chapter, what should we as a church do next?

The questions for group study include the following:

1. Has your church entered a period of belt-tightening?

2. Has your church been unable to meet its budget projections in three or more of the past five years?

3. Have large swings in income occurred over the past two years?

4. In two or more of the past five years, have your budgetary projections been attained only after appeals for special financial gifts from the congregation and/or leaders?

5. Do you plan budgets that are based upon some benefactor riding to the rescue with a large gift? If so, how does that make you feel? Do you feel more content? Or does it add a sense of uncertainty, discomfort, and insecurity? Can you create budgets that do not rely on gifts of benefactors? Why or why not? And if not, what could be done to change this?

6. Have church staff members left or been asked to leave in the past two years, in part because of budgetary constraints and/or cutbacks?

7. Is confusion, discord, and/or dissent rising due in part to the leaving of staff members?

8. Does your church have savings of any kind (such as savings accounts, stocks, endowed investments, bonds)? Compare the ratio of your savings to your operating expenditures and charitable/missionary giving. If it is not in an 80-10-10 ratio, what is the ratio?

   Place your answer here: _____ – _____ – _____
   (operating budget–charitable giving–savings)

9. If you have an investment and/or savings, do you tap into the body of this investment or only into the return on it? Do you want to change this? Should you change this? And if you want to make a change, when and how could you bring this about?

10. Who are the people involved in creating and overseeing your budget? Do they represent a balance between forward thinkers and realists? Next ask yourself, What did Aaron Wildavsky mean when he said a budget was a "plan" *and* a "prediction"? Has your budget been operating as a plan? Has your budget been operating as a prediction?

CHAPTER 5

Missteps with New Facilities

We shape our buildings: thereafter they shape us.
—Winston Churchill, British statesman and prime minister[1]

Factors That Cause Initial Growth in Churches	Erroneous Decisions That Lead to Plateauing	Corrective Steps to Regain Initial Growth
Rented or renovated facilities are cost-effective, flexible, and multifunctional.	Dramatic increase in overhead is due to newly purchased or constructed facilities. In addition, these facilities are often segregated into activity-specific spaces (i.e., immovable pews in an auditorium, small Sunday school rooms that cannot open up into larger quarters, etc.).	Utilize the "Seven Dos When Building a Facility" outlined in chapter 5, including renting or remaining longer than you think you need to. Doing this will place hardship upon your staff, but increase your financial viability and future flexibility. It will also create flexibility in your facilities. Then when it is time to build, employ architects who build malls, colleges, and theaters, not those who primarily build churches.

How Facilities Can Stop Growth

"None of us could figure out the cause of our attendance decline, but to me, it has always seemed to have to do with this building."

The church facility was scarcely nine years old. Its setting was idyllic and serene, encased by rows of trees and surrounded by subdivisions of expensive homes. To many congregations, this is the church they dream about: clean, modern, and securely situated in an upscale section of the community.

But the church was dying. Nine years earlier, more than 3,800 people worshiped in rented facilities. Now, fewer than 900 attended the church, and on weekends the sanctuary (built to seat 4,500) felt cold and bare. The pastor who had led the congregation for nineteen years had recently left.

"Joel [the former pastor] just got too frustrated," began Tim, a lay leader. "He couldn't figure out what went wrong, so he blamed himself. None of us could figure out the cause of our attendance decline, but to me, it has always seemed to have to do with this building." After more discussion, it appeared Tim's analysis was correct.

Mount Sinai Church had begun growing about two years after Joel arrived. Formerly a plateaued church, the church slowly embraced new ideas with Joel's help. Soon the facility was too small to house the growing congregation. The facility was renovated two times, and a nearby school and community center were utilized. Similarly, an empty downtown store housed the youth ministry. Then when the church's sanctuary became too small, the church reduplicated its services at different times. When that became insufficient, the leaders rented a local gymnasium for services. Under those circumstances the church had sped along quite contentedly with significant growth. "For me those were the best days," recalled Tim. "Everything we did seemed to be blessed by God. And then it all fell apart."

Money had been readily available, and existing facilities were cramped and cumbersome. Thus, the leaders decided to aggressively pursue a new facility. Within one year an architect/builder had been hired. "We toured a lot of churches that were the size we wanted to become," recalled Tim. "And we chose an architect whose buildings seemed innovative, but still looked like a church." The architect/builder suggested the church was on a growth curve that required a 4,500-seat sanctuary, reckoning that the combined total of the church's four Sunday services was almost 3,800.

The lay leaders were responsible for the location. It was a peaceful section of town, adjacent to a growing subdivision. The community's most desirable elementary school was nearby. Everyone agreed that though somewhat off the beaten track, it was the location where they all would love to live and worship.

Less than eighteen months after the congregation moved into the new facility, growth plateaued. Then over the next two years, growth declined. Finally after four more years of decline, the pastor resigned, heartbroken over the waning attendance and unable to understand the forces involved. The church was on the verge of bankruptcy. Although a weekly attendance of nine hundred would be a sizable congregation for most churches, for this church it was inadequate to pay the mortgage.

Factors That Caused Initial Growth

There were three notable causes of growth in Mount Sinai Church.

Cause of Growth #1: Initially, growth had been driven in part by the availability of funds to launch new ministries and hire new staff. As we saw in chapter 4, financial flexibility allows a church to adapt more quickly to community needs. Driven by the rapidly increasing attendance, the leaders used their mushrooming budget to hire more staff, renovate the facilities, and start new ministries. The fiscal freedom contributed to flexibility, satisfaction, and growth.

Cause of Growth #2: The location of the original facility, on a corner of a busy city street, had been a plus. Many people knew Mount Sinai Church because they passed by it daily. Rented youth facilities in the downtown area further increased community awareness. And because the church services were eventually held in the local school auditorium, the church advertised heavily in the media. All of this created a community awareness for the church, which in turn resulted in increased visitor flow.

Cause of Growth #3: When the facilities were renovated early in the growth cycle, multifunctional space was intentionally created. In the renovated sanctuary pews were eschewed in lieu of movable seating. Walls were removed to link classrooms, allowing them to be utilized for larger gatherings. Everywhere around the cramped and confined facility, multifunctional and flexible spaces were created.

Erroneous Decisions That Led to Plateauing

At Mount Sinai Church, erroneous decisions beset the leaders as they made plans to build. Under the tutelage of an architect/builder of other large church facilities, they made erroneous missteps that soon stunted their growth and eventually reversed it. Their missteps may be categorized into seven "don'ts."

Seven Don'ts When Building a Facility

Error 1: Don't build too soon. Oftentimes a rented or paid-for facility will be less expensive to operate than a new facility. Though architects may laud cost savings of new facilities, the new facilities may require large unforeseen expenditures. Repairing a boiler in an existing facility might cost $8,000 to $10,000. In a new facility of the same size, the cost might be twice to three times that amount. Although a builder/architect may suggest that would not happen for years, it happened within the first five years at Mount Sinai. Thus, building cautiously and patiently can help generate a fiscal reserve.

Error 2: Don't build too big. On the advice of their architect/builder and based upon their own overly optimistic projections, the church leaders built a facility that was oversized for their congregation and their budget. We saw in chapter 2 how multiple weekend celebrations can give the church more options for attracting community residents. And the four Sunday services at Mount Sinai provided this benefit. Yet naively, the leaders decided to hold one large combined church service in the new facility. Thus, robbing the Sunday services of their flexibility and convenience, they undermined their attendance. "We all agreed we wanted everyone together, and only one service was the way to do it," recollected Tim. "But we didn't expect such a drop-off in attendance."

Error 3: Don't build without flexibility. Renovated and rented facilities had given Mount Sinai Church needed flexibility. If the church needed to change usage or space requirements, the leaders could rent a different site. In addition, because of the cramped facilities, multifunctional areas were mandated. But when the new facility was built, many ministries were segregated into activity-specific spaces. Immovable pews were installed in the auditorium, and small classrooms were designed, separated by load-bearing cement walls. Since church members were tired of years of cramped and communal space, they tried to give everyone an area in the new facility. "The groups were going to have their own rooms at last," mused Tim. But creating these private enclaves weakened the flexibility that had contributed to growth.

Error 4: Don't use a plateaued church for your model. Mount Sinai's leaders had visited several seemingly successful churches in the region. Unfortunately, they did not ask if the churches were plateaued or declining. Of the five churches they visited, two were declining and two were plateaued, but their impressive facilities kept Mount Sinai's leaders from looking closer. The architect/builder who had designed the lone growing church was rejected, in Tim's words, as "too wild for us; it looks like a mall."

Error 5: Don't build in a detached location. The building site was an area where many leaders would have liked to live and worship. But unlike their first facility (and the rented spaces downtown), it lacked visibility. "It was on a moderately traveled road," suggested Tim. "But it was across town from the main highway. I really wish we had built adjacent to Route 20." Visibility is one key to outreach. Unfortunately, churches often link their destiny to a parcel of land that is convenient for current attendees, but in a detached location that slows or undercuts growth.

Error 6: Don't forget to seek information from the right experts. Church leaders thought they were getting the best advice available when they hired the architect/builder of another large and prestigious church. In fact, he had built dozens of churches. But because most of the churches in America are declining or plateaued, the architect/builder was inadvertently experienced in building facilities that contributed to church plateaus and/or declinations.

Error 7: Don't expect new facilities to increase the church's attendance. Related to errors two and six, this must be mentioned again because it is so prevalent in the sales pitch of many architects/builders. As I noted earlier, Christians are an optimistic lot. In my experience architects/builders succumb to this malady just as easily. Together they can give overly aggressive projections. "The architect advised us on church growth projections. He said a new facility would increase our attendance by 10 to 15 percent," recalled Tim. "He said they were based on his company's history. But now I question his figures." While architects and builders are experts in legal codes and civil engineering, few are acquainted with the principles and strategies of church growth.

Corrective Steps to Regain Growth

Seven Dos When Building a Facility

Each of the seven errors has a positive alternative.

Corrective Step #1: Do wait longer than you think you should before you build. Waiting can help you further define your needs and objectives. Patience also allows fiscal swings to moderate and more precise financial projections to be created.

More money can be set aside for savings as well. Finally, cautious and unhurried behavior allows you to plan your future more precisely.

Corrective Step #2: Do build a smaller-sized auditorium, leaving room for expansion. Creating spaces where everyone can worship simultaneously may not be needed (combined "unity" gatherings can be held in rented facilities)[2] or wise (we saw in chapter 2 that multiple celebration options allow a church to reach a greater percentage of a community).

Corrective Step #3: Do create flexibility in your facility to compensate for the smaller size. Though a smaller facility can cause tension and minor friction, it can lead to creativity. And sharing facilities forces an expanding congregation to interact and work out this conflict, thus creating interaction between potentially divisive groups.[3] Designing flexible spaces also provides adaptability for future programming.

Corrective Step #4: Do use a larger, but *growing* church as your model. Don't let impressive facilities and/or reputations dissuade you from discovering if your model church is growing. Ask yourself, Does the architect/builder build growing churches or plateaued/declining ones? In addition, ask the architect/builder for references, and interview former clients. Ask the references if they feel the facilities have hindered growth to any degree.

Corrective Step #5: Do build in a visible location. For unchurched and dechurched people, accessibility is essential. Robert Schuller tells how fellow clergypersons extended to him their condolences when he could find no facility to rent other than a drive-in theater. "Don't feel sorry for me," Schuller replied. "The Orange Drive-In Theatre is right on the Santa Ana Freeway, and that's the heaviest traveled road in the State of California. . . . Nobody has a better road leading up to their front door than I do! And you have to have a road leading up to your front door before you need a building."[4]

Corrective Step #6: Do get advice from the right experts. Seek out architects/builders who build malls, theaters, and colleges rather than churches. Churches are often designed with a formulaic look and inadequate flexibility. Here I cannot fault architects/builders too much. Most of their church building experience revolves around aging congregations, who are building smaller facilities or merging. These architects have little experience with facilities that foster connectedness and growth. Today, the architects of malls and shopping centers are becoming the designers of connectedness in America. Malls have replaced the streets of small town America as the venue for meeting people and building relationships. One young teenager confided, "It's at the mall where I feel at home with my friends. There's a coffee bar, comfortable couches, TVs, a fountain, and lots of people hanging out. It sure beats church." Unfortunately, the church is being beat by the sense of community created by many retail environments. Where once it was said, "I met my spouse at church," too often today it is heard, "I met my spouse at the mall."

Corrective Step #7: Do plan on the size of your congregation plateauing or declining moderately after a building project. Change always brings about tension, and as a result, polarization between the status quo and change proponents often erupts.[5] But because change is unavoidable, tension will be encountered. Therefore, the tension involved in moving into new facilities does not usually grow a church. Because some people find this change especially jarring, they look for a congregation more in keeping with their former church experience. Thus, a decline should be anticipated in budget and usage projections. Hiring an expert in church growth can be expeditious for realistic planning. The American Society for Church Growth (www.ascg.org) lists dozens of church growth consultants trained and skilled in helping churches navigate the precipitous waters of growth, change, and facility expansion.

A SUCCESS STORY

Point of Grace Church, West Des Moines, Iowa: Building Innovation into Your Facilities

"Each one of your 'Seven Dos When Building a Facility' we did; we just didn't have a list," exclaimed Jeff Mullen, pastor of a rapidly growing church with a facility that supports flexibility and innovation.

"Here is what people will see, hear, and feel when they come to Point of Grace Church for the first time," began Jeff. "We're situated on the busiest road in the area, so they won't have trouble finding us. About four miles away they can tune in their radios to our radio station, which prepares them for the worship experience with music and church news. When they get to the facility, they will drive past our large glass atrium and be directed to ample parking. As they walk up to the facility, they will hear the same worship music they heard on the radio coming from hidden outdoor speakers.

"When they enter the facility, they will continue to hear this music without interruption. And it will feel as if they are walking into an upscale mall. Concierge desks are directly ahead, and on the left is the early childhood area where parents can drop off their children. On the right is our glass atrium, which looks like an upscale food court at a mall with a fireplace, comfortable seating, and a coffee/juice bar. In all of these areas there are more than thirty plasma screens playing worship music. You see, we want to acquaint people with worship slowly, but intentionally as they enter the facilities.

"As Christian leaders, we have to ask ourselves, Where do normal people hang out? They hang out in normal places, like malls and movie theaters. Churches usually build abnormal places, and they expect normal people to fit. When you force normal people into abnormal spaces, you put them off. Here the whole mood and atmosphere work together to prepare them for the good news.

"Before we moved, we had two services with a combined attendance of 1,200. But in our new facility we have three services. A lot of architects were telling us to build a 1,200- to 1,500-seat auditorium. But to reach people, you must hold multiple services. So our new auditorium seats 750, a size attendees were already used to.

"To compensate we have three auditoriums now because flexibility is the rule around here. In my fifteen years of ministry, I've led services for thirteen years in schools. And frankly, newer schools have better traffic flow and gathering areas.

"Our main auditorium seats 750, and it is built like a modern college classroom, or a movie theater, with stadium seating. I think there is something psychologically intimidating about looking up at a stage. With stadium seating our worship leaders are down at the bottom. The audience doesn't look up at them; they look down upon them as their servants. And you can press a button and the risers retract into the wall and you have an auditorium for basketball or whatever.

"Behind the auditorium is a large backstage area. Most churches just have a brick wall, opening to the outside. That will kill your flexibility. We have a huge door that opens to technology rooms, rehearsal rooms, staging areas, a green room, and also leads to the backstage area of our Kid's Stuff Theatre. Here we run a musical theater program for kids and their parents. The adults sit on chairs and the children sit on the floor, and we present the good news in an energetic way. The theater can be used for all sorts of programs and seats 350.

"The third area is our atrium, a food court and gathering area with glass walls. It will seat 450 around tables. We can hold services of different styles here or use it for overflow from the existing sanctuary. It is a real multipurpose room for the western suburbs. That's why we call it the Event Center. It can be used by the community for weddings, anniversary parties, corporate gatherings, and so forth. As you can see, we have large, medium, and small auditoriums.

"Our architect, David Price of ChurchWorks™, has an unbelievable ability to create community in comfortable places.[6] His family has a history of working with the Walt Disney organization, and he really knows how to make people feel that church can be the happiest place on earth. And church should be!

"To sum up, the church has to engage and embrace folks who are exploring the truth of Jesus Christ for the first time. To do that, we have to meet them on their turf. Thus, we want our church to remind them of a place they would normally go. To them when they visit our church, it still feels that they are on their own turf. When we treat people this way, we honor and respect them. The gospel is not necessarily comfortable, but the environment should be."

QUESTIONS FOR GROUP STUDY

The following questions are for group study:

1. Have you experienced a plateau or decline within the five years after a building project? If so, can you brainstorm five causes? For each cause, what could have been done differently?

2. Have you experienced pastoral turnover within the five years after a building project? If so, can you list several causes? For each cause, what could have been done differently?

3. Review the "Seven Don'ts When Building a Facility" in this chapter. Which "don'ts" have you experienced? What should you have done differently?

4. Now, review the "Seven Dos When Building a Facility." Which "dos" have you (or should you) experience? Make a list of action steps that you will undertake (with due dates attached) in order to employ each of these "dos."

5. If you have hired or are going to hire an architect, have you or will you ask the following questions?

   - Of the churches you have designed and/or built, what is the Average Annual Growth Rate[7] of those churches in each of the ten years before and after the facility was built?
   - Are you experiencing a polarization between the people in your church who want to bring about change and those who want to keep things the way they have been?[8]

CHAPTER 6

Missteps with Innovation

*I cannot help fearing that men may reach a point where they
look on every new theory as a danger, every innovation
as a toilsome trouble.*
—Alexis de Tocqueville, French social philosopher[1]

Factors That Cause Initial Growth in Churches	Erroneous Decisions That Lead to Plateauing	Corrective Steps to Regain Initial Growth
Experimentation is encouraged. Almost all theologically noncompromising ideas are considered.	The church begins to stay with "what has worked in the past," even if that is the immediate past. This often leads to incipient traditionalism.	Foster an environment of experimentation and exploration. Rapid changes in cultural predilections and preferences require this.

Headed Down in Uptown

*"Then we zeroed in on a few things that worked, and did
less and less creative stuff."*

The church was in the trendy Uptown area of Minneapolis. Surrounded by art galleries and boutiques, its location in a renovated art deco theater seemed fitting. "Come look at this," beckoned Kerry. Exiting the theater foyer, we climbed a wrought iron staircase to the church offices. "This is my pride and joy," Kerry continued. "It's the award for entrepreneur of the year from the Uptown businesses. This award symbolizes the first seven years of Laury Park Church. Because we tried everything and anything to minister to this community. Yet we never compromised the gospel.

"But then we zeroed in on a few things that worked, and did less and less creative stuff. When I look back now, our growth stopped about the time our creativity stopped."

Though there were other causal factors, Laury Park Church's innovative ministries played a key role in reaching the creative personality of its Uptown neighbors.

In Which Environs Does Innovation Work Best?

While creative innovation works well in most environs, it is necessary in some. In communities like Uptown, where young professionals under the age of forty-five make up a sizable portion of the populace, creativity is essential. In many upscale suburbs where wealthy residents have diverse experiences and inclinations, creativity is a must. And finally, creativity usually is preferred by communities that are economically disenfranchised. In such locales, creativity and innovation become a favored outlet for community residents to express their gifts and talents. Historically, most of our innovative musical and art forms originate from such locales.

Doesn't Innovation Create Too Broad a Ministry Focus?

On the surface, creating new ministries seems to go against the strategy of sticking with a narrow range of ministries that line up with your church personality as reflected in your philosophy of ministry.[2] But new ministries can be kept within a specific range that aligns with your church personality. And in chapter 7 we will see how evaluation can help end ineffective programming. Thus, creativity becomes necessary to provide replacements. While it is important to line up programs with your personality, it is equally important to experiment and vary programs within that range to maintain constancy and freshness.[3]

Factors That Caused Initial Growth

Innovation was an important factor in the growth of the church in Uptown.

Cause of Growth #1: Innovation was viewed as part of the church's personality. As we have seen, staying true to your church personality (as reflected in a philosophy of ministry) is imperative. If your community responds favorably to innovation (as most do), then innovation needs to become a central part of your church character. This not only attracts community members, but also helps keep a focus on and an expansion of innovation.

Cause of Growth #2: Innovation kept the good news fresh. Though the message will never lose its efficacy, the medium through which it is transmitted may. In other words, while God's Word will never lose its power, the programs we employ to share it may wane in effectiveness because of changing cultural preferences.[4] For example, the revival meetings of the early part of the twentieth century did not attract the young people of the latter half of the century. However, under other formats and names (e.g., concert, rally, rave), evangelistic events have flourished today. In addition, prayer meetings have been revived as concerts of prayer by adopting a format attractive to younger generations and using the term concert, a word younger generations understand. The new believer's class has been replaced by the highly effective Alpha Course in which a basic orientation to Christianity is taught in a manner that is understandable by younger generations. In all of these strategies, the content has not changed, but the method of delivery has been creatively updated.[5]

Cause of Growth #3: Innovation allowed new forms of ministry to emerge. Innovation owes its genesis to experimentation. Most of our traditional forms of ministry were once experimental (and often controversial). Innovation allows original and fresh approaches to develop.

Cause of Growth #4: Innovation energized people. In the first half of the twentieth century, researchers looked at how to motivate workers. Elton Mayo was a leader in this field, and he discovered that people could be motivated by change. Workers worked harder and more happily when something about their workplace changed. Even something as trivial as changing the color of the room increased employee performance. All because newness, freshness, and adjustment keep people from becoming bored and less productive.[6]

Cause of Growth #5: Innovation honored God. Creativity is a reflection of a Creator who glories in the originality of his handiwork. As Isaiah said, "Lift your eyes and look to the heavens: Who created all these? He who brings out the starry host one by one, and calls them each by name. Because of his great power and mighty strength, not one of them is missing" (Isa. 40:26). In addition, the European cathedrals of the Middle Ages hired only the best craftsmen in each trade so that when they were completed (some taking more than five hundred years to finish), the cathedrals became testimonies to people's God-given gifts of innovation and creativity. The flying buttress, pointed arch, and rose window are a few of the architectural innovations created by craftsmen seeking to honor God with their skill and creativity.

Erroneous Decisions That Led to Plateauing

The following errors contributed to the plateau and eventual demise of the church in Uptown:

Error 1: The church stuck with the creative things done in the past. Because of the magnitude of the task, and because programs had so recently been innovative, the Uptown church chose to stick with what had worked in the past. Though that appeared to be the safe course, that choice detached the church from the innovative community surrounding it.

Error 2: People expected innovation from the Uptown church. The innovative ministries of Uptown Church had become a hallmark in the minds of community residents. The church's shift to "what has worked in the past," even the recent past, signaled to the community an increasingly derivative and unimaginative approach to ministry.

Error 3: Creativity was too money and labor intensive.
While retaining old programming can appear cost-effective on
the surface, a lack of innovation can undermine enthusiasm and
relevance. A slowing in the growth of excitement, attendance,
and fiscal income usually results. And thus, as the business world
has learned, it is too costly not to innovate.

**Error 4: Staying the course can steer a church into incipient
traditionalism.** Traditional forms of liturgy, ministry, and administration were once innovative. The Protestant Reformation ush-
ered in singing in indigenous languages and accompanied it by the
technological wonder of the day—the pipe organ. Innovators continually broke with the past to revitalize ministry. But too often and
too soon, these innovations become codified into traditions. Today
this problem can beset even young and innovative churches.

Corrective Steps to Regain Growth

Instead of Entrepreneur—Innovator!

Herb Miller, in his examination of successful church leaders,
declared that they are "entrepreneurs." [7] However, there are competing definitions for entrepreneur. In the management field Peter
Drucker has tendered the most accepted definition, that "innovation is the specific function of entrepreneurship."[8] In other words,
creativity and innovation are the key traits that distinguish who is
an entrepreneur. Therefore, to become entrepreneurs, we must
study how to engender innovation and creativity.

Creativity is a process that employs three general phases, with
specific steps for each. The three stages are preparation, illumination, and verification.

Stage 1: Preparation

To begin the creative process, preparation is essential. Here are
three steps:

**Corrective Step #1: Decide to explore new opportunities
rather than disparage them.** In *Good to Great,* Jim Collins

discovered that people take one of two views toward cultural shifts and styles. Either they castigate them, building up a defensive position and decry them, or they inquisitively investigate them. This is not to say that all opportunities are appropriate or even theologically defensible. But leaders who inquisitively examine innovation can separate the good from the godless and then creatively engage culture.

Corrective Step #2: Be wary of your bias toward the concrete. A natural tendency is to prefer what is working now, or has worked in the past, over what might work in the future. "Concrete" evidence of past or present productivity usually overshadows unseen or untried potentials. Miguel de Cervantes in *Don Quixote* wrote, "A bird in the hand is worth two in the bush."[9] And this has been the motto for many churches. However, successful organizations overcome their concreteness bias and regularly field-test new options and ideas.[10]

Corrective Step #3: Admit you do not know as much as people think. With success often comes the feeling of expertise and an imperviousness to missteps. However, researchers have found that successful leaders admit their limitations and weaknesses, leading to flexibility and willingness to think in creative ways.[11] In addition, psychologist Theresa Amabile discovered that successful leaders are more tolerant of ambiguity, for a longer period of time.[12] The result is that imaginative ideas are given the opportunity to incubate and bloom.

Stage 2: Illumination Through Buildup and Breakthrough

The next stage requires what David S. Landes describes as a "buildup" in knowledge on the subject and then a "breakthrough" to a decision.[13]

Corrective Step #4: Build up your knowledge base, and then let it incubate. Leaders may dive into strategy formation without a sufficient knowledge of the issue. Begin with personal research on the topic, and then let the ideas incubate through reflective thought.[14] Doing this also allows time for God to comment through inner promptings. Researchers have discovered that creativity declines when deadlines loom or when a leader creates a "hurry up" environment.[15]

Corrective Step #5: Use small groups to increase creativity. Together a group of creative people will typically make more creative decisions than each would on his or her own. This phenomenon is called group polarization, for groups tend to shift or polarize toward more extreme viewpoints.[16] This works in the reverse as well, in that convening a small group of conservative thinkers will usually elicit a more conservative decision than group participants would suggest on their own. Use this phenomenon to your advantage. If you are seeking highly imaginative ideas, convene a group of your most creative thinkers. Since creativity is in short supply, it might be wise to pool creative minds to draw out the most innovative solutions feasible. In addition, prepare group participants to expect some tension and conflict. American social philosopher Eric Hoffer said, "The most gifted members of the human species are at their creative best when they cannot have their way."[17]

Corrective Step #6: Use brainstorming. In 1938 Alex Osborn invented brainstorming as a way for his advertising agency to think creatively. A uniqueness of this strategy is that it guards "against being both critical and creative at one and the same time." [18] These are the five rules of brainstorming:

(1) There will be no discussion of the ideas until after the brainstorming process.
(2) The more options the better.
(3) All ideas are welcome.
(4) Combinations of options are sought.
(5) Proposing or hearing an option does not mean accepting it. [19]

The following are the four steps of brainstorming:

(1) The leader describes the problem.
(2) Group members share their ideas. Clarification is allowed, but no one is allowed to criticize. Everyone withholds judgment until all alternatives have been heard.

(3) Group members are encouraged to be as innovative and radical as possible. Remember, proposing an option does not mean accepting it. Group members are also encouraged to piggy-back on other participants' suggestions.

(4) Only when all alternatives have been suggested do group members debate the merits of each.[20]

Brainstorming caveats. Sometimes timid members will be hesitant to share novel ideas for fear of criticism. This can be overcome by utilizing one of the following variations on brainstorming:

Electronic brainstorming. This is identical to brainstorming, but the group convenes electronically over the Internet where participants remain anonymous. Studies show that this type of brainstorming can outperform face-to-face brainstorming sessions in the number of ideas generated.[21]

Nominative Group Technique (NGT). In this version of brainstorming, group members write down their ideas.

(1) The leader describes the problem, allowing thirty to forty minutes for each group member to write down ideas and solutions.

(2) The leader reads their anonymous solutions to the group. No criticism or evaluation is allowed.

(3) Alternatives are discussed in the order they were proposed.

(4) When all alternatives have been discussed, each participant ranks each, and the highest ranking is chosen.[22]

Corrective Step #7: Converge on a solution. Leaders must guard against the temptation to analyze options so long that they outlast their applicability. Evaluate all alternatives, allowing respectful debate on the merits and limitations of each approach. Then, trim down your options. Finally, gain consensus and agree upon the most suitable course of action.

Stage 3: Verification

As we will see in the next chapter, evaluation is a critical part of any strategy. Here are some brief thoughts about verification:

Corrective Step #8: Don't be afraid to qualitatively and quantitatively evaluative programming. For an in-depth discussion, see chapter 7.

Corrective Step #9: Don't become discouraged by failure—but enjoy surprises. Peter Block, in *The Answer to How Is Yes,* states, "When something doesn't work, they [creative leaders] find it somewhat interesting, much like scientists."[23] This inquisitive nature, and a refusal to be disheartened by failure, characterizes creative minds. In fact, surprises, both good and bad, fuel the creative person's enthusiasm. Warren Bennis and Robert Thomas remark, "As the process of problem solving floods the person's brain with pleasure-giving endorphins, dealing creatively with the problem becomes both motivator and reward."[24]

Corrective Step #10: Enjoy your creative capital. Capital means a surplus, and a church that is launching creative and innovative ministries will create a surplus of good feelings about innovation. *The New York Times* reported in "Economic Evolution: From Making to Thinking" that workers today take pride primarily in the creative thinking, complex problem solving, and collaboration that go into their work.[25] This overflow of good feelings for those served, as well as those serving, can be a significant motivator.

A SUCCESS STORY

The Creative Life of Life Church, Edmond, Oklahoma City, Tulsa, and Stillwater, Oklahoma

Craig Groeschel is the senior pastor of Life Church, a congregation affiliated with the Evangelical Covenant Church, which has four campuses in Oklahoma. Craig holds a bachelor's degree in marketing, as well as a master of divinity degree. The church began in 1996 with a handful of people, and by 2003 the church was ministering to more than seven thousand people each weekend through ten worship options. I asked Craig, "How do you maintain innovation as your church grows?"

"That's a great question because it's one of the biggest dangers for churches. First, we have to be willing to do things that make us uncomfortable, and maybe even things that we don't like. For example, we have one worship experience that I personally would not go to. But we have more people come to Christ at that celebration than at any of the others. It is creatively out of my comfort zone, but it is very, very effective.

"Second, we have to continually bring new voices to the table. These are people that can bring fresh ideas. And we do it through our creativity team. It's necessary because the longer we do something, the more we become comfortable with it. And soon something that was once nontraditional becomes a tradition. We get stuck in a rut. When I started out, I was the young guy around here. And now, seven or eight years later, I am not as up-to-date with what is going on out there. Thus, you have to bring new voices to a table.

"And then third, we must be willing to take calculated risks. When we start off, we regularly take faith risks because we have nothing else to fall back on. But once we get something that works, it's easy to just keep doing it. We stop taking those faith risks to reach people."

"Can you elaborate a bit more on the role of your creative team?" I queried.

"We've put together a department known as the 'creative team' to advise us how to stay contemporary in everything we do," replied Craig. "They study what the world is doing on everything from MTV to the latest movies. They try to keep a fresh perspective on what is happening out there. Their sole ministry is to bring creativity to every ministry within the church. They look at every upcoming event, program, and ministry and suggest to its leaders ways to make it more creative and engaging. Whether it's a kids' presentation, something for single adults, missions, or youth, they brainstorm about it and help the leaders give it a look, a design, and maybe even creative videos. And they serve me greatly. Every teaching series I do, they help give it a look, a personality, and a life of its own. They come to me with all sorts of wild ideas—that wind up being great. Their ideas help give my messages a modern edge that the unchurched person can relate to."

"Is your creativity team comprised of laypeople or staff?" I asked.

"Both, but when we first started, they were just volunteers. One staff member went out and recruited people. And they got together once a week for brainstorming sessions."

"Did your background in marketing help?"

"It probably did. But what really drove me was that though I grew up as a church kid, I never got it. Looking back, I'd have to say, 'Hey, you guys never grabbed my attention.' Therefore, I want to make sure that we grab people's attention. They won't hear the message until we engage them."

"Is there one last approach that you would like to pass along to a church that is being tempted to stick with what has worked in the immediate past?" I asked.

"I would tell them to have a one-month ministry fast," said Craig. "Just stop doing ministry the way you have been doing it, and force yourself to come up with something different. That's worked for us. We get in seasonal ruts where we do the same thing for three or four months. So, we'll just say, 'During the next four to six weeks, we're not going to do it that way anymore. We're going to find some new way to do it.' Boy, that shakes people up! But when you take a thirty-day fast from what you've been doing, it forces you to look outside of your box."

QUESTIONS FOR GROUP STUDY

The following questions are for group study:

1. Is creativity or innovation one of your church traits? If so, how? And if not, why not?

2. Is an emphasis on innovation and/or creativity characteristic of businesses in your community? Why or why not?

3. Which generations in your community might be best reached by creativity and innovation?

4. Would any impact you might have on your community be worth the discomfort and difficulty of employing a new approach?

5. What are some new approaches that have been talked about? List them on the left side of a sheet of paper. Now, in the right column, answer the following questions:

    - What would be the advantage and disadvantage of each?
    - What are some sacred beliefs about how you operate that might be challenged by each?
    - What impact could each have on your organization?
    - What impact could each have on your community?
    - Is it worth the effort?[26]

6. Have you employed the type of nonjudgmental brainstorming or NGT sessions that this chapter describes? If not, or if it has been a while, reread the section on brainstorming. If it is warranted, schedule a session.

CHAPTER 7

Missteps with Evaluation

*Unless strategy evaluation is performed seriously and
systematically, and unless strategists are willing to act
on the results, energy will be used up defending yesterday.*
—Peter Drucker, management consultant and author[1]

Factors That Cause Initial Growth in Churches	Erroneous Decisions That Lead to Plateauing	Corrective Steps to Regain Initial Growth
Housecleaning occurs. Ideas that don't work are quickly abandoned. Limited resources and the precariousness of the church's survival create this situation.	Programs and ideas that may not be productive are given extra time "to develop." Jesus' parable on repentance (Luke 13:1-9) is often misapplied to rationalize extending the life of an unproductive program.	Be prepared to use vigorous analysis and empirical evidence to confirm productive programming. Often supporting evidence of a program's viability is anecdotal. Look for clear evidence of productivity (James 3:17).

Sinking in a Morass of Ministry

*"We've got more ministries than we can afford to fund or
run. We've traded one morass for another."*

"Look at this," the pastor began, handing me an 11-by-14-inch
flowchart of the church's ministry. Though only three years old,

the church had a tangled web of ministries and programs that could rival a long-established congregation. "We started this church to get away from the top-heavy and ineffectual programs of churches we used to attend. Now we mirror them. And we can't cut anything because everything has its defenders. So, when a new idea comes up, we just add it rather than ending something. It seems we're bloated, and our volunteers are getting burned out. We need to get lean and mean."

Gerry's estimation was not far off target. Though pushing more than 160 in weekend attendance, the church's growth was slowing due in part to waning enthusiasm among the volunteers. "We've all been here before," added Janice, a lay volunteer and head of the church council. "We started the church so we could focus on ministries that people wanted." "But now, we've got more ministries than we can afford to fund or run," interjected Gerry. "We've traded one morass for another. Jesus tells a parable about patiently fertilizing a fig tree to see if it will eventually bloom, and we've used that passage to rationalize a lot of unproductive programs. And now, it seems that we've got more fertilizer than growth."

Lynwood Community Church began only three years before, with a great deal of enthusiasm among its volunteers. But now a lack of evaluation threatened to overwhelm the church with programming and burn out its leaders. In addition, the pessimistic attitude of the leaders was beginning to scare off new recruits.

Factors That Caused Initial Growth

Lynwood's leaders were excited about starting with a clean slate. As a result, they inaugurated ministries they knew would be effective in reaching their friends and neighbors. And soon Lynwood began to quickly add attendees. The following are some factors that contributed to the initial growth of Lynwood Community Church:

Cause of Growth #1: Programs were chosen based on effectiveness. When a new church is started, a blank slate allows the leaders to experiment with innovative programs. And because time, energy, and money are at a premium, only the programs that show clear and direct potential are utilized. As a result, innovative programs with the greatest potential for success are selected.

Cause of Growth #2: A small number of programs dominated the church's ministry focus. A narrow focus in programming allowed church members, as well as their guests, to easily define the focus and personality of the church. Although the leaders did not have a philosophy of ministry or personality statement (though they could have), the narrow concentration of its programming helped everyone, volunteer and guest alike, to remain focused on the church's mission and direction.

Cause of Growth #3: Programs that were not clearly effective were summarily ended (that is, housecleaning occurred). The leaders looked for progress in Christian maturity along with numerical and financial growth to validate a program's usefulness. If one or more of these characteristics was not evident, the idea was quickly abandoned. The precarious nature of a church in renewal or initiation means that congregants are less tolerant and patient with nonproductive programming.

Erroneous Decisions That Led to Plateauing

Christians tend to be tolerant and lenient with people as well as with the ideas that they introduce. However, this tendency toward patience can cause unproductive programming to continue beyond its use and/or purpose. The following are several errors that often establish, and sometimes even ritualize, unproductive programming:

Error 1: Leaders relied on information cascades.[2] Leaders may adopt strategies without first evaluating their suitability, simply because the strategy works for another congregation. This often occurs when attendees of seminars or workshops return enthused about a new and fashionable idea. As a result, because this new idea appears to work elsewhere, information about it "cascades" upon or "deluges" the leaders of the congregation. And they feel helpless to ignore this onslaught of enthusiasm or to scrutinize it for suitability. Adopting an idea that everyone appears to be utilizing seems prudent because it saves time and other valuable resources. But giving in to information cascades can lead to poor decisions that are based on unevaluated and potentially unsuitable information.[3]

Error 2: Leaders used biblical rationale to preserve unproductive programming. Jesus' parable in Luke 13:1-9 is often cited as a rationale for extending the life of unproductive programming. In this parable, Jesus tells of a man who digs around an unproductive fig tree to fertilize it in hopes that it will yet bear fruit. This passage may be quoted when requesting additional time and/or resources for unproductive programming to prove its fruitfulness. However, the context of Luke 13:1-9 reveals that Jesus is describing God's graciousness in allowing unfruitful persons extra time before judgment. Misapplying this scripture can quickly create a foundation for rationalizing unproductive programming.

Error 3: An abundance of programs gave the church a feeling of success. Comparing themselves with larger churches they hoped to one day become, Lynwood's leaders began to take pride in their expanding range of ministries. As a result, they added ministries that were too labor intensive for their size or not in keeping with their personality and character.

Corrective Steps to Regain Growth

A Three-stage Process for Analyzing Program Effectiveness

Analyzing the effectiveness of a program or ministry is not widely practiced in churches, but it has biblical validation. James makes such an admonition in James 3:17, asserting that divinely inspired ministry will be "full of . . . good fruit," that is, laden with productivity. Ensuring this productivity includes a three-stage process with corresponding corrective steps.

Stage 1: Ensure that each ministry and program lines up with your philosophy of ministry.

Programming should support and advance your church's personality as reflected in your philosophy of ministry. In fact, a good philosophy of ministry or personality statement will readily tell you whether or not a ministry fits your congregational character. Before evaluation begins, you must create this standard by which to judge program and ministry effectiveness. For more information on the content and creation of a philosophy of ministry, see chapter 2. Then use Corrective Steps #1 and #2 to ensure your assessment is conducted by an appropriate supervisory group.

Corrective Step #1: Encourage broad participation from all segments of the congregation on committees assigned to regularly, but graciously, evaluate programming. Evaluation is necessary, but it must be handled by a compassionate, yet analytical group assembled from a broad spectrum of the church. Often existing administrative councils will be too polarized and/or politicized to serve in this function. At these times, it will be helpful to inaugurate an assessment team or committee to review the productivity and suitability of programming.

Corrective Step #2: Be prepared to surrender personal ministry preferences and predilections for the overall good of the congregation. Attachment to a ministry is commonplace, especially for those involved in a ministry's inception. Still others may have greatly benefited by a program and thus be highly protective of it. However, ministry programs can decrease or even cease in effectiveness over time. At such junctures leaders with personal attachments to programs need to step back and surrender their predilections to the corporate good.

Stage 2: Compare the results you expected with your actual results.

Use Corrective Steps #3 to #5 to critique your results, both anticipated and actual.

Corrective Step #3: Be the first to get the bad news. Leaders should seek regular and informal feedback, especially negative feedback. However, because people are wary of the "kill the messenger" syndrome, leaders are often the last to hear bad news. Management writer Harvey Mackay cautions leaders, "You'll always get the good news; it's how quickly you get the bad news that counts."[4] The following are key locales in which to get both positive and negative feedback:

Venue 1: Your Church Corridors. Harvey Mackay recalls how the former head of the Dayton-Hudson Department Store Group (now the Target Corporation) regularly took the department store elevator to his ninth-floor office.[5] On the elevator he repeatedly interacted with customers and thus kept his pulse on how his store was doing. In the church context, this venue might be the church corridors. Casually frequenting these corridors allows casual conversations to develop.

Venue 2: Your Newcomers. Speak with church newcomers. Leaders should be actively involved in newcomer meetings and courses so that newcomers can become acquainted with the leaders and the leaders can get to know them.[6]

Venue 3: Your Neighborhood. As you encounter people in the community, do not force conversations to take this evaluative tack, but allow conversations to naturally flow toward insights you could gain from community residents.

In each venue, ask people one of these questions:

- "What can we as a church do better?"
- "What are the needs of people your age that we should address?"
- "Could you tell me some improvements we could make at _____ (*church name*)?"

In *Unnatural Leadership*, Dotlich and Cairo tell how they often gather a leader's team in a room and have the leader ask, "What can I do better?" The leader then leaves the room. "The leader's team, armed with flip chart and marker, then answers the questions in detail and shares the answer with this executive."[7] Dotlich and Cairo note that while many leaders might find this too uncomfortable, the benefit of getting potent feedback is immeasurable.

Corrective Step #4: Use facts, statistics, and measurable goals to evaluate programming.[8] By looking at measurable and numerical productivity, along with the three other types of church growth described in the next step, we can gain important statistical verification instead of verification that is typically anecdotal.

Corrective Step #5: Evaluate all four types of church growth.[9] Four types of church growth are found in the book of Acts.

Maturation Growth. In Acts 2, Christians were growing in maturity, as demonstrated by their desire to devote "themselves to the apostles' teaching and to the fellowship, to the breaking of bread and to prayer" (Acts 2:42). Ministries can be evaluated in part by the degree to which they are producing disciples who seek out and engage in these spiritual disciplines.[10]

Growth in Unity. As the disciples grew in maturity, they began sharing their possessions in acts of interdependence and reliance. They "were together and had everything in common" (Acts 2:44), even though the pooling of fiscal resources was not the norm for all or even most New Testament churches. But the unity and harmony that these actions signify are essential. Effective programming should be expected to generate inter-reliance and concord.

Growth in Favor. Acts 2:47*b* indicates that the early church was "enjoying the favor of all the people." Effective programming should be meeting community needs, and thus eliciting community favor and approval. Community gratitude and approval can be "a powerful conduit through which the good news flows into a community."[11]

Growth in Numbers. An outgrowth of the three types of qualitative growth just described should be quantitative growth. In other words, numerical growth should accompany growth in quality, as is attested in Acts 2:47*c* where "the Lord added to their number daily those who were being saved."

Numerical growth receives most of the attention, but it is only *one* type of growth that should be expected and measured. Therefore, evaluation that seeks to ascertain appropriateness of programming must be careful to analyze and critique *all four* elements of church growth.

Stage 3: Take corrective actions to ensure results conform to your plans.

Consult the following corrective actions for ways to merge, revitalize, or terminate unproductive programming:

Corrective Step #6: Nonproductive ministries do not always need to be discarded; sometimes they only need to be renovated. When a ministry clearly lines up with a church's philosophy of ministry, and obvious strategies for reformation exist, abandonment may not be required.

Corrective Step #7: Sometimes it is advantageous to combine and/or merge ministries. Many times as ministries grow, they shift their focus, and eventually, two or more ministries may grow similarly in scope and focus. When this occurs, consider merging these ministries into a new combined structure. Though doing this can revitalize a ministry, it is sometimes challenging because of perceived fiefdoms. Nevertheless, merger is a key tool in the process of sustaining productivity.

Corrective Step #8: Do not be afraid to deliberately, but delicately, terminate, spin off, or give away nonproductive programming. This step may be the hardest one of all. In a needy world, it is difficult to think of ending a ministry. But we are stewards of God's people and their resources, and as a result, we are required to address nonproductive ministry. Though certain programming does not fit your church personality, it may be viable in another context or venue. Thus, intentionally but gracefully move toward ending nonproductive and/or nonaligning ministries by giving them away to another church/ministry, spinning off an independent program, or if need be, bringing them to a close.[12]

A SUCCESS STORY

Willow Park Church, Kelowna, British Columbia, Canada:
Evangelism, Edification, Equipping—and Evaluation

Mark Burch is the senior pastor of a Mennonite Brethren church that was averaging 817 in attendance in the year 2000, but in 2003 was reaching more than 1,550 each weekend. The success, according to John Baergen, executive director of the Leadership Centre

Willow Creek Canada, occurred because "they evaluate continually, putting necessary people and resources behind key and/or emerging ministries."[13] To find out more, I spoke with Mark.

"We begin by looking to see if what we are doing is supporting our mission. Our mission is 'leading people to follow Jesus,'" stated Mark. "And we talk about doing this through three ministry avenues. Officially we have three churchy terms, *evangelism—edification—equipping*, but we usually say they equal other, more modern terms.

"**First, *evangelism* equals 'connecting.'** I know some people have problems with this, but we evaluate a lot of programming by the numbers. That means we look at how many people get saved in outreach programs. We had eighty-two conversions in the first five months of this year. And we put roses for adults and balloons for children on the altar when people make a commitment to Christ. It creates excitement. People are always looking to see if there are balloons or roses up there. And our dear older people have had to put up with a lot of new, modern music. But one said to me, 'Pastor, as long as there are roses in the front of the church, you go ahead and sing that weird music.'

"**Next, we focus on *edification*, which equals 'growing.'** This is much harder to gauge. But we offer discipleship courses with graduated designations, such as Discipleship 101, Discipleship 201, and Discipleship 301. We keep track of how many people are progressing through each course. And we regularly ask our staff, 'Are your programs providing opportunities for people to learn?'

"**Finally, *equipping* we translate as 'serving.'** We go through our database and see who isn't involved in ministry. We contact them and help them go through a spiritual gifts inventory or meet with them to find out what their gifts are.

"We also look at how each of our programs lines up with our five core values:

1. **Bible teaching.** Everything has to be centered around the Word. We want to make sure that all programming is biblically centered and helping people fall in love with God through the treasures of the Word.

2. **Christ exalting.** We worship by living out our Christian lifestyle in the community. We look at all of our programs and ask ourselves, 'Does it help us be more Christlike with the people we live among?'
3. **People empowering.** This is based on Ephesians 4:12. We ask, 'How effective is your program in raising up new leaders?' And 'If you weren't here next week, would the ministry you oversee keep going?'
4. **Community building.** Because we are a growing church, we have to keep the small church feel by using small groups. We always want to know how effectively a ministry is creating small group opportunities.
5. **Mission motivating.** Finally, we want to make sure everything we do motivates people to support the Great Commission of Matthew 28:19 to reach the unchurched.

"So we evaluate everything through a grid of three ministry avenues and five core values. When we look at things this way, it's pretty easy to see what doesn't line up. And if some program doesn't line up, we aren't afraid to end it. We're fallible people, and we make mistakes. And we're not afraid to say that. It's okay to fail here. But most of the time . . . we seem to succeed."

Questions for Group Study

The following questions are for group study:

1. Do you have a philosophy of ministry? If not, this is your starting place for evaluation. Return to chapter 2, and read how to create and deploy a philosophy of ministry (i.e., personality statement).

2. Do you regularly evaluate your programming for effectiveness? If so, is the process sufficient? If not, what should you do? Reread the corrective steps in this chapter to inaugurate

the three-part process for evaluating programming effectiveness.

3. When was the last time you asked people how the church was doing in the following venues?
Your church corridors _____ *(date)*
Your newcomers _____ *(date)*
Your community _____ *(date)*

How often do you think you should poll these people in the future? And what do you think should be the results? Finally, decide to whom and when you will report the results.

4. If you have nonproductive programming, ask yourself the following question:

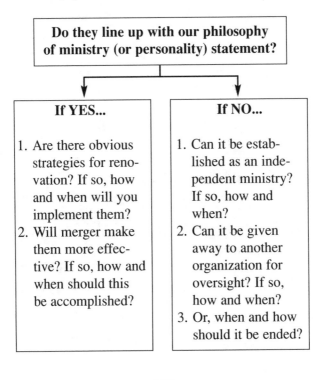

Do they line up with our philosophy of ministry (or personality) statement?

If YES...

1. Are there obvious strategies for renovation? If so, how and when will you implement them?
2. Will merger make them more effective? If so, how and when should this be accomplished?

If NO...

1. Can it be established as an independent ministry? If so, how and when?
2. Can it be given away to another organization for oversight? If so, how and when?
3. Or, when and how should it be ended?

CHAPTER 8

Missteps with Dysfunctional People

Stopped churches . . . must now break out of their middle-class encirclements, seek receptive peoples in their neighborhoods, and establish constellations of living congregations among the masses.
—Donald A. McGavran, dean of the Church Growth Movement[1]

Factors That Cause Initial Growth in Churches	Erroneous Decisions That Lead to Plateauing	Corrective Steps to Regain Initial Growth
Dysfunctional people become functional. All people, regardless of physical, social, or economic dysfunction, are actively recruited. Prior leadership experience in another church is not required.	Functionally adept people are actively recruited. Prior leadership experience in another church is highly valued. Unproductive programming is often unintentionally cross-pollinated.	Utilize small groups and a lay-training system to mentor dysfunctional people into functional and productive lives in both church and society.

How Success Stopped Church Growth

"In the beginning we needed leaders . . . any leader."

The congregation was moving into a new facility in a popular suburb, but the senior pastor was not going. Darren had grown up in a tough section of this metropolitan area. And as a young adult, he had participated in the gang and drug culture of his neighborhood.

But in his twenties, he became a Christian, and sensing a call to the ministry, he volunteered at nearby First Church.

Now Darren was leaving the ministry. As he prepared to reenter the business world, he reminisced about the changes that had taken place over the past eleven years. "Because we weren't given a chance to be leaders at First Church," he began, "we started our own church. But no one imagined we'd become First Church."

Darren felt First Church did not seriously consider him for the opportunities he longed for in leadership and pastorship. Thus, after two years, he and other like-minded young people left First Church to start their own ministry. Two group homes were established to reach out to the many disenchanted youth of the neighborhood, and before long a church emerged.

The church began a consistent growth curve and eventually purchased a downtown theater. "But as we grew," continued Darren, "we distanced ourselves from the people who started the church. In the beginning we needed leaders . . . any leader. So we recruited street people, ex-druggies, people with a lot of baggage. And, boy, did they come up with creative ideas to reach their friends. And the ideas worked!

"But as we grew to over five hundred, leadership seemed too important to entrust to them. So, we hired people with experience in other churches, with educations, and professionals from the business world. And they brought a lot of churchy programs that people in the neighborhood couldn't relate to. Eventually, our leaders didn't reflect our congregation, and we stopped growing.

"At that time we began hemorrhaging people. New churches were started up out of our congregation without permission. I could relate to their frustration because I had felt the same way at First Church, that leadership was off-limits. Looking back, I see that the congregation was unhappy with the direction our 'professionals' were leading.

"When it became clear we couldn't afford the theater anymore, we bought land where most of our leaders came from . . . the suburbs."

I asked why he decided to leave now. He replied, "It's not the church I started . . . it's First Church."

Factors That Caused Initial Growth

When I interviewed leaders who had been present since the church's inception, most felt that a gradual change in the church's focus was to blame. At first the church had, by necessity, developed its leaders from the only resource available: the socially, physically, and/or economically dysfunctional people who populated the neighborhood. In fact, the local media had published several stories about how the ragtag band of former street kids now led a growing church. And the media attention drove more disenfranchised people to their doorstep.

But with growth in size and stature grew smugness and aloofness to their roots. Plus, the daunting task of running a growing church that passed five hundred in attendance necessitated hiring people with experience. Thus, a chasm between ministers and those ministered to eventually contributed to a halt in growth.

Out of interviews emerged the following factors that had driven their initial growth:

Cause of Growth #1: Dysfunctional people were made functional (i.e., "redemption and lift"). Because the pool from which the church drew its leadership was primarily composed of dysfunctional people, the church excelled at helping the maladjusted and socially estranged become well adjusted and stable individuals and leaders. Jesus himself modeled this ministry in his selection of common fishermen, political collaborators, and social outcasts as his disciples (Matt. 4:18-22; 9:9). Donald McGavran suggested that this results in "redemption and lift," for in the foreign mission field he observed that spiritual "redemption" led to a rise or "lift" in social stature, maturity, and responsibility.[2] Seeming to confirm this, Paul reminded the Corinthian church, "Brothers, think of what you were when you were called. Not many of you were wise by human standards; not many were influential; not many were of noble birth. But God chose the foolish things of the world to shame the wise; God chose the weak things of the world to shame the strong" (1 Cor. 1:26-27).

Cause of Growth #2: The leaders understood the people they sought to reach. Because only years earlier they had been involved in the drug and gang culture of their community, the indigenous leaders understood their neighborhood well enough to employ innovative and effective outreach strategies. "We held block parties where we would give out clothes. We had a giant benevolence fund to help people who were out of work. We held alley-way Bible studies during the day for [drug] dealers. We were radical in our approach! Though we baffled First Church, people on the streets could tell we cared," remembered Darren.

Cause of Growth #3: No one was overlooked. Because there was a leadership shortage, no one—no matter how disenfranchised or unstable—was overlooked. The group homes, which had been the precursors of the church, were established to cultivate leadership through a Christian home environment, an environment many of them had never before experienced. Thus, no matter how inappropriate the background, there were a clear route and a genuine opportunity to become a leader.

Cause of Growth #4: There were no limits. Anyone, no matter what his or her background, could rise to any level in leadership. After all, the senior pastor had once been a drug abuser.

Cause of Growth #5: There was a sense of celebration due to a clear supernatural participation in the redemption of people. It was evident that the church's strategic thinkers had been social outcasts only years before. And this intrigued the media as they reported on how Christianity had emancipated and lifted these individuals. As a result, the congregation and the community celebrated God's unmistakable participation. "We weren't ashamed of our past because it's what makes us real. People could relate to us," recalled the pastor. "And no one could deny God did it!"

Erroneous Decisions That Led to Plateauing

After the purchase of a downtown theater, the church appeared successful and stable. As a result, growth mushroomed to more than 1,100. But the burgeoning attendance also attracted a different type of leader. Leaders from other big congregations began to solicit employment.

Simultaneously, because of the size of the congregation, the leaders began stressing competence and expertise over willingness. Slowly, the church leaders, both lay and clergy, came to be comprised of an increasing number of well-educated, veteran church leaders. As a result, a gap emerged between the leaders and the congregants. As we saw in chapter 1, this problem often besets growing churches. But here the chasm was exacerbated by the social gulf between the highly educated new leaders and the rank-and-file attendee who was still somewhat socially disenfranchised and/or estranged.

The following are errors to which the church inadvertently succumbed:

Error 1: Expertise was preferred over willingness. The size of the congregation, and thus the magnitude of the task, began to eliminate neophytes and novices from leadership consideration. "The work was too important to put in the hands of raw recruits," remembered Darren. "I'm sure glad God didn't feel that way when we were getting started."

Error 2: Dysfunctional people were seen as only the mission field instead of the mission field *and* the leadership pool. Socially disenfranchised people were still the target of the church's outreach, but the leadership recruits were drawn from outside their ranks. Again, the work was seen as too important to entrust to neophytes.

Error 3: Unproductive programs were unintentionally cross-pollinated. Veteran leaders brought with them unproductive programs and tactics from their former church environments. The innovative and pioneering strategies that had characterized the church in its early years were now deemed too radical or extreme for the new congregational stature. Thus, the church's ministries unwittingly started to mirror other sizable, but plateaued, congregations.

Error 4: Celebration of redemption was replaced with a celebration of expertise. The church now began to revel in the experienced and prominent leaders who were being drawn to the church. Rather than jubilation over redemption, euphoria over expertise became customary.

Error 5: The socially estranged attendees viewed the new leadership as either rescuer or persecutor. The gentrification of the leadership created a feeling among the average congregants that the leadership should rescue them out of their woes, or that the leadership was holding them back. Thus, a social chasm began to widen between the leaders and the attendees.

Corrective Steps to Regain Growth

Six Steps for Developing Indigenous Leaders

As with all of the corrective steps in this book, the solution lies in recovering the forces that led to growth in the first place and redeploying them. The following corrective steps can help implement that process:

Corrective Step #1: Ensure that discipleship takes place in small groups. The group homes had been an incubator for discipleship and the development of leadership. The forces of maturation, accountability, and harmony that are unleashed in small groups are amazing. Little wonder Jesus employed a small group as his primary incubator for discipleship (Matt. 10:1-5; 11:1). Therefore, do not rely on outside education solely; rather, employ small training groups to acquaint new leaders with the regimens and requirements of leadership.

Corrective Step #2: Ensure that there are no limits. Knowing that God can use anyone, and that there exists no glass ceiling in leadership development, can inspire and motivate potential leaders. Rather than accent the expertise and education of your leaders, extol the "redemption and lift" your leaders have received.

Corrective Step #3: Mind the gap that emerges between leader and follower. "Mind the gap," a phrase borrowed from Britain's warning to subway riders, here reminds us that a gap will naturally emerge between leaders and their constituents. Ensure that leaders stay connected to their mission field and do not inadvertently poke fun at, scorn, or deride a sordid background. While wrongdoing should never be lauded, the redemptive power that has taken the person from offender to leader should be extolled.

Corrective Step #4. Take care that leaders do not become viewed as either rescuers or persecutors. A triangle can be used to demonstrate how victims often categorize those who reach out to them as either "rescuers" or "persecutors."[3] A rescuer is one who acts on the victim's behalf, doing what the victim cannot or does not want to do. This leads to dependency on the rescuer and eventually the social system. The other possibility is that the victim will view the person reaching out as a "persecutor" who is also holding the victim back from reaching his or her potential. This creates animosity toward the social system. Regrettably, to make sense of their environment, victims often categorize those reaching out to them as either rescuers or persecutors. Figure 8.1 demonstrates this triangle.

Figure 8.1 How Victims Often See Those Who Reach Out to Them

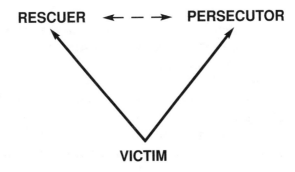

Figure 8.2, on the other hand, demonstrates what I call the Whitesel Triangle, for in it I propose another link, halfway between persecutor and rescuer, which I have labeled mentor. In this preferable outcome the mentor operates halfway between rescuer and persecutor, never becoming either but adopting the

best attributes of both to coach and critique the victim into a place of wholeness. Churches that continue to mentor social outcasts will ensure that they remain connected with, and effectively reach, their local mission field.

Figure 8.2 How Victims Should See Those Who Reach Out to Them

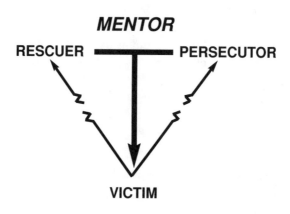

MENTOR

RESCUER **PERSECUTOR**

VICTIM

Corrective Step #5: Offer a clear route for leadership training, employing a mixture of courses, small groups, and laboratories. "In the early days when we had our Leadership Institute," observed Darren, "it was basically weekly Bible classes. But they had to have sixteen courses to graduate. And some of our best leaders came from it." Leadership development is one of the most underemployed strategies in growing a church. Here are key elements for developing leadership training:

(*a*) Develop "job descriptions" for all positions. These should include qualifications, time limits, accountability channels, and explanations of what is expected for "acceptable," "good," and "outstanding" performance. Job descriptions allow potential recruits to quickly understand the nature and scope of a position.

(*b*) Offer a series of leadership courses aimed at training new leaders. Many people are afraid to volunteer because they feel unqualified. A regular leadership training institute (even one night a week) can alleviate this malady. Courses that employ Bible study along with Christian and secular leadership books will be beneficial.

(*c*) Use courses that build upon one another. Colleges designate courses by ascending numbers to specify the level of expertise required. Thus, Management 101 would be of a more introductory nature than Management 425. Use such course designations to help emerging leaders see that leadership development is a continuing process, and that once they complete prerequisites, they can progress to more complex courses in leadership.

Corrective Step #6: Recognize that this lesson is for every church. Even though your church may not have been built upon dysfunctional people becoming functional, all churches have the spiritual commission to redeem and lift the socially estranged. No greater model need be cited than Jesus' earthly ministry and the disciples he called.

A SUCCESS STORY

New Life Fellowship, Queens, New York:
Cultivating Leaders in Queens

"Once I changed my outlook, we exploded in size. And now the driving force of our church is to be 'a quality multiethnic church, that reaches, equips, and releases indigenous leadership.' "

Transcribing notes from an interview with Pete Scazzero can be daunting. The only thing that flows faster than Pete's words is his mind. But from this man gushes forth authentic enthusiasm for shaping disenfranchised people into responsible disciples and eventually leaders.

Pete pastors New Life Fellowship, a multiethnic church in Queens, New York, which is weekly reaching more than one thousand people. They also have seven other churches that are part of the New Life movement. And though they have moved into a renovated $10 million building, "the building or numbers on a Sunday morning are not my focus," contended Pete. "My focus is mentoring new leaders.

"I have totally lived the missteps you are talking about," continued Pete. "I believed the myth that to grow, you had to have experienced staff. So I brought in from the outside the best staff I could find. It was a disaster! They didn't understand the church or culture.

"About seven years ago I recognized how flawed my thinking was. I was still under the delusion that if I could bring in some great worship guy, this church would grow faster. Our local worship guy was a great leader. But I think I was blinded to his potential because he wasn't dynamic. I secretly felt he would fill the gap until I could get someone else.

"But it changed my thinking when I studied the biblical example of a farmer. You don't farm or grow a church overnight. It's a slow process, and so is developing church leadership. Eventually, the music guy grew into a great leader and mentor. And to many, he is the rock of our church."

Pete's approach also centers on ministering spiritually and emotionally to the leader. His book *The Emotionally Healthy Church* explains why emotional health is as important as leadership skill.[4] "I want a leader to be healthy at home and at church," stated Pete. "Therefore, we begin our leadership process with a combination of emotional and spiritual training.

"We start with courses on the basics of Christianity, coupled with participation in a small group. People grow emotionally in small groups, and that's just as important to us as leadership skills. At the same time, we offer graduated levels of leadership courses, including what we call Equipping Courses, In-depth Bible Discovery Weekends, Personal Formation Seminars, along with general leadership training.

"Once I changed my outlook, we exploded in size. And now the driving force of our church is to be 'a quality multiethnic church that reaches, equips, and releases indigenous leadership.' It's not a quick fix. You won't get an overnight church. But you will get quality, indigenous leadership . . . and a stronger, healthier, more mature church."

QUESTIONS FOR GROUP STUDY

The following questions are for group study:

1. What is the ratio of leaders that were developed from within your church, and those that were developed in other churches or organizations? Write in the ratios:

   ____ (leaders developed from within your local church)
   ____ (leaders developed from outside your local church)

   If the top ratio is less than 50 percent, you may have an impediment to indigenous leadership development. Reread Corrective Step #5.

2. How do the leaders of your church mirror your mission field? Are they of the same social, financial, geographic, and/or educational levels? If not, which variables have diverged? If this is the case, what should be done?

3. Do you utilize job descriptions to acquaint volunteers with opportunities?

   - If so, how often are they updated? And how often are they deployed?
   - And if not, what could be the benefits of writing and utilizing job descriptions?

   If you do not employ job descriptions regularly or extensively, make an action plan to correct this.

4. Do you host leadership training classes for emerging leaders? If so, how often? If you do not offer at least one course a quarter,

and are averaging more than 150 in weekend attendance, you are thwarting emerging leaders. Take action steps to implement leadership training at least once a quarter. Solicit topics from the congregation.

5. If you do offer leadership training, to whom do you target these opportunities? If you heavily recruit your existing leaders, you may be burning them out with too many requirements. Existing leaders are usually overworked and eschew the thought of having to undertake more training. After all, they reason, they have been educated by the school of hard knocks. Thus, focus most of your leadership training toward people not yet involved. Your goal is to add new leaders, not run off existing volunteers.

CHAPTER 9

Missteps with Staff Education

I can say without affectation that I belong to the Russian convict world no less . . . than I do to Russian literature. I got my education there.
—Alexander Solzhenitsyn, Russian dissenter and author[1]

Factors That Cause Initial Growth in Churches	Erroneous Decisions That Lead to Plateauing	Corrective Steps to Regain Initial Growth
Staff members have low educational experience in their ministry fields. Thus, they do what they intuitively "sense" or "feel" is right. Plus, new ideas are generated from the constituency they serve.	Staff members become trained in the "classical" fields of theology, Christian education, church music, and ministry. These newly acquired skills are probably those that are practiced in influential but plateaued churches. In addition, new ideas are increasingly generated from professional colleagues instead of constituents.	Embrace 50/50 learning. Learning engendered in the "classical" milieu of seminaries, workshops, and Bible colleges must be balanced by 50% of the learning coming from practical and alternative sources, such as nonaccredited institutes (e.g., the Wagner Institute), workshops, field experience, and secular opportunities.

The Surprising Effectiveness of Nonseminary-trained Leaders

*"The twentieth century continues to verify the trend, the
most innovative, rapidly growing churches still relying
upon untrained clergy."*

In this chapter I will digress from commencing with an amal-
gamated church illustration and interview a secular researcher in
the field of church growth. Roger Finke is professor of sociology
and religious studies at Pennsylvania State University, as well as
director of the American Religion Data Archive. Roger seeks to
use science, history, and mathematics to understand why
churches grow and decline.

"What is the primary effect of staff education on church
growth?" I began.

"As we look at American church growth over the past two hundred years," replied Roger, "we see a startling fact: that relatively
untrained clergy continue to be far more effective in bringing
people into the church than those trained in most seminaries.
Nonseminary clergy tend to be simply more enthusiastic for the
gospel, they understand their congregants better, and they are
more responsive to the needs of people they seek to reach.

"These observations are based upon statistical trends, surveys,
and denominational reports from over two hundred years of
American church history.[2] For example, the most rapid period of
growth for Southern Baptist churches clearly occurred when they
were relying on clergy not trained in the seminary, but rather
recruiting pastors from the neighbors and friends of the people
they served.

"And with the Methodist churches the trend is even clearer.
They grew the fastest in the nineteenth century when they had
circuit riding pastors without seminary training, lay preachers,
and lay leadership directing the local class societies. Once they
stressed seminary education, the circuit rider was dismounted,
and rather than training under the tutelage of an experienced
mentor, he or she went to seminary. A very rapid shift to decline
coincided.

"The twentieth century continues to verify the trend, with the most innovative, rapidly growing churches still relying upon untrained clergy, like the Vineyard Fellowships, Calvary Chapels, and Harvest Fellowships.

"This occurs for two reasons. First, when seminary-trained leaders look to implement new ideas, they usually turn to their network of professional clergy for ideas and programs. As a result, seminary-trained clergy are less likely to employ innovative and indigenous approaches. But untrained leaders are usually more innovative, for they have to rely on another network: the people in the community, businesspeople they work with, and newly converted people. As a result, they constantly introduce more creative, experimental, and effective models.[3]

"Second, in my research with Kevin Dougherty we found those who are seminary trained tend to be less involved in daily Bible reading, and devote fewer hours to prayer than their non-seminary counterparts. We found that the key is the degree to which a seminary emphasizes spiritual and biblical formation. Spiritual formation includes inculcating the traditional and biblical strengths of the denomination, along with high biblical standards, moral values, a vibrant prayer life, optimism, and so forth. Some seminaries are offering this, and seminarians who go there retain a spiritual fervor similar to clergy with no seminary training.[4]

"Conrad Cherry in *Hurrying Toward Zion* found another factor affecting spiritual formation. He discovered that seminaries that have little consensus of belief among the faculty, and that encourage students to embrace a critical, almost skeptical spirit, do not foster spiritual formation among their seminarians.[5] It is hard to develop spiritual formation when there is not a consensus on what one's beliefs should be.

"Don't get me wrong, it doesn't mean you shouldn't go to seminary. But seminary training must include spiritual discipline as well as academic rigor, and the gospel must be celebrated as well as critiqued. When seminaries stress academic training in lieu of spiritual formation, the position of the pastor becomes a profession . . . and not a calling."

Factors That Caused Initial Growth

In this chapter, the factors that contributed to growth, along with the erroneous decisions that led to plateauing, parallel those in the previous chapter, albeit for different reasons. Thus, the following overview in this chapter will be more concise:

Cause of Growth #1: Leaders remained in touch with their mission field. Christian leadership skills often develop best in a mission field rife with tensions, temptations, and spiritual confrontations. In such scenarios leaders learn on the job, gaining valuable firsthand experience on how to handle unpredictable and daunting situations.

Cause of Growth #2: Learning on site increased availability. This is a win-win situation for the church and the learner. The church benefits from leadership that is not furloughed for further education while the learner benefits from consistency and practicality.

Cause of Growth #3: Innovation was more likely to occur in a laboratory rather than a classroom environment. Learning is more deeply inculcated, as well as creativity more common, when the learner can immediately deploy and then adjust strategies in a laboratory environment overseen by a mentor. Some seminaries, but not all, focus primarily on the classroom as learning theater. What little practical opportunities are offered may not provide adequate oversight.

Cause of Growth #4: Local issues took precedence over national issues. In many seminaries the touchy theological issues that are contested on a national level take center stage. This is in part because seminary professors are often conscripted to address denominational-wide issues of significance. This is not to say these are unimportant issues. But a focus on national issues often overshadows the seminarian's opportunity to tackle local issues that have greater significance for the seminarian's local constituency.

Cause of Growth #5: Learners did what "seemed right" or what they intuitively felt should be done. This reliance upon Holy Spirit–guided field adaptability and innovation launches creative avenues for ministry. Largely unaware of the traditional and/or typical strategies, street-level leaders lean heavily on the guidance of the Holy Spirit, their background, their constituency, and their intuition.

Erroneous Decisions That Led to Plateauing

Erroneous decisions might have included the following:

Error 1: An individual was considered to receive the best education in a prestigious learning environment. Prestigious educators and environs may be necessary for those on the track of theological pedantry, but for the effective local leader, a laboratory that closely approximates his or her eventual mission field is to be preferred.

Error 2: Spiritual formation was not stressed adequately in some seminary environments. As Finke and Dougherty discovered, some seminaries do not sufficiently stress spiritual formation, including practical biblical methodology, moral values, a vibrant prayer life, optimism, and so forth. In addition, some seminaries do not offer laboratory environments where future ministers can hone their skills under the care of a skilled mentor.

Error 3: Questions were engendered rather than solutions. This is related to Error 2, for we saw from Conrad Cherry's research, seminaries that have little consensus of belief, and that encourage students to embrace a critical, almost skeptical tone, do not usually foster spiritual formation among their seminarians. As Finke noted, "It is hard to develop spiritual formation when there is not a consensus on what one's beliefs should be."

Error 4: Leaders might focus on national issues that polarize and/or are irrelevant to their local constituents. When pastors invoke discussions on national and often divisive topics, the local constituency may feel estranged because these issues may pale alongside pressing local and personal concerns.

Error 5: Intellectualism took precedence over skill development. Theologian H. Richard Niebuhr tendered a reasonably widespread perspective on the seminary as *"the intellectual* *center of the church's life,"* where "subjects of love, faith and hope must be set somewhat at the fringe of awareness."[6] In such a cerebral setting, emotional needs and skills can be overlooked in lieu of intellectual development.

Corrective Steps to Regain Growth

Embrace 50/50 Learning

The expression 50/50 learning denotes organizations and strategies that embrace a balance between theory and practice (and though they may not always be in a ratio of 50 percent to 50 percent, they are proportionally balanced for the milieu). Let's examine six corrective steps that can foster a 50/50 strategy:

Corrective Step #1: Embrace 50/50 learning between theological and practical opportunities. "Classical" training in theology and polity is important, but it must be balanced with practical strategies that will help a leader effectively influence the community.

Corrective Step #2: Embrace 50/50 training between local and national issues. Sometimes national issues can become so strategic to the future of the denomination that a pastor feels compelled to address them on a repeated basis. However, if national concerns are not balanced with an equal emphasis on local issues and needs, the leader may distance himself or herself from the ministry field.[7]

Corrective Step #3: Embrace field and secular experience, along with seminars, workshops, nonaccredited institutions, and roundtable discussions to attain a 50/50 balance in training. Many pastors are already well versed with the theoretical and theological finer points of their vocation. Therefore, these individuals should seek out secular and field experiences, as well as seminars, nonaccredited schools, workshops, and caucuses, that engender practical skills.

Corrective Step #4: Embrace distance education to foster 50/50 learning. Rather than leave the confines of the local mission field, students are discovering that so-called distance learning can take place over the Internet and/or through semiregular forays to academic environments. No longer is it necessary to spend three or more consecutive years away from a student's future mission field to obtain an education.

Corrective Step #5: Embrace seminaries that practice 50/50 learning. A growing number of seminaries stress practical as well as theoretical training. However, successful programs must include conscientious oversight and mentoring of their laboratory experiences. Thoroughly examine schools to determine the practicality and success of their approach. Representatives from five seminaries that are on the vanguard of 50/50 learning are interviewed at the end of this chapter.

Corrective Step #6: Embrace 50/50 learning between spiritual and intellectual formation. Disciplining the mind to grasp and dissect great theological issues must be balanced with an environment that promotes spiritual growth and discipline. Carefully investigate the efficacy by which training venues emphasize and cultivate spiritual formation and disciplines in their attendees.

Five Seminary Leaders on 50/50 Learning

"We want to make sure the passion that students bring here will increase during seminary. Schools can very easily put a damper on the passion."

The following is an overview of discussions with leaders of five seminaries that are probing the nexus of theological training, spiritual formation, and practical learning. Dr. Jules Glanzer is dean of George Fox Evangelical Seminary, Dr. Randy MacFarland is vice president and dean at Denver Seminary, Dr. Richard Peace is Robert Boyd Munger Professor of Evangelism and Spiritual Formation at Fuller Theological Seminary, Dr. John Walt is vice president of community life at Asbury Theological Seminary, and Dr. Steve Wilkes is professor of missions at Mid-America Baptist Seminary.

"All of your schools have long and illustrious histories of theological education," I began. "But what are you doing to give practical training to your seminarians?"

"Here is how our system works," responded Randy MacFarland from Denver Seminary. "When students enter our Master of Divinity program, they are introduced to our eight ministry Training Centers. They are not buildings but networks of mentors and ministries in particular contexts. The contexts are chaplaincy, church planting, counseling, suburban, urban, missions, rural, and campus. Students meet with various Training Center directors to decide which is the best fit in light of God's call. You see, if a person's call is to urban ministry, then it is imperative he or she be put in an urban context and be mentored by urban leaders during seminary education. Our Training Center directors are well networked with churches ministering in the director's area of expertise, and help the seminarians get involved with local churches and ministries to practice their ministry."

"How do you maintain oversight?" I asked.

"Four mentors give oversight," continued Randy. "The Training Center director, the ministry professional mentor [a minister in the church the seminarian is serving], a lay mentor, and a faculty mentor. The faculty mentor also serves as the facilitator of the seminarian's weekly spiritual formation group. It counts as part of the teaching load of that professor. The spiritual formation group includes up to ten seminarians who covenant together for encouragement, accountability, and worship. Plus, the student meets one hour each week with two of the other three mentors to gauge progress, spiritual formation, and skill development.

"But goals are important too. So, every semester the seminarian writes two learning contracts. One learning contract addresses character or spiritual formation, and the other contract is in an area of competency or skill development. For each contract seminarians are required to invest 60 hours a semester to receive 1 hour of credit. When they graduate, they have received 10 hours of credit and 600 hours in the areas of spiritual formation and skill development."

"We're developing the same thing," added John Walt from Asbury. "We're creating a small group laboratory, based upon each student's interest in ministry. We will have ten to twelve options, so a seminarian can concentrate on evangelism, mercy/justice, homeless ministry, campus ministry, and so forth. The seminarian will partner with other interested students, and a professor skilled in this area of ministry will mentor each group."

"At Fuller we have hands-on laboratory environments in many courses," stated Richard Peace. "For example, in a course on church research methods, each student learns how to collect data from community surveys, the Internet, and personal interviews . . . by actually getting out there and doing it. And in my course on small group evangelism each small group of students designs and hosts a small group outreach event to share the good news with seeker friends. Practically every faculty member has courses along this line."

Steve Wilkes of Mid-America Baptist Seminary added, "We also want to equip seminarians to share their faith in a personal and courteous way. So we ask students to talk about their faith with someone every week, and report on this activity. And we travel on regular trips to Mexico, Ecuador, Brazil, and Russia where seminarians share their faith in factories, hospitals, and on the street. It is amazing the closeness and spiritual growth you experience when you are comfortable sharing your faith."

"And what are you doing to counteract what researchers Finke and Dougherty call a statistically verifiable conclusion that 'those who are seminary trained tend to be less involved in daily Bible reading, and devote fewer hours to prayer than their nonseminary counterparts'?"[8] I asked.

"At George Fox the spiritual formation of students is our highest priority. If a student hasn't experienced transformation during his or her seminary experience, we feel we have failed," noted Jules Glanzer. "Students take a spiritual formation course every semester in their program, in protected time slots, so that they do not conflict with required classes. Twenty-five courses range from the traditional such as Prayer and Spiritual Life to the specialized such as Spiritual Formation and Social Justice, Images of

God, Spirituality and the Cosmos, and Spiritual Formation and the Senses. And each has content, discussion, reflection, and small group accountability. However God might be moving in a student's life, we have a course that will maximize that growth."

"Spiritual formation is right at the top of the agenda at Fuller," stated Richard. "Not only do students and faculty pray before classes, but more spiritual formation courses are being offered all the time, with weekly Bible study, prayer, and reflection a part of the course agenda. And a growing number of courses are including weekend prayer retreats as part of their curriculum. In addition, we have a number of students who daily spend an hour in prayer, Bible study, and meditation, using the Ignatian material. They then meet weekly with a small group to process and deepen that material. And once a month they meet for individual sessions with a spiritual director. This is a nine-month program and commitment."

"At Asbury," affirmed John, "we use our daily chapel service as a learning laboratory. Our chapel worship is dynamically alive. At the end of every chapel service, we minister to each other at the altar, student-on-student and student-on-professor. We stress they are not joining a seminary, but rather a 'kingdom demonstration plot.' It's a place were your spiritual life is focused upon, as well as given freedom to be expressed. Therefore, we have prayer chapels in every building on the campus. And we encourage students to block out an hour a week in solitude talking with the Lord."

"In summation," Randy noted, "these things we are talking about are absolutely critical. I don't see how we can train leaders without addressing the spiritual formation of the leaders along with the skills necessary to be successful in ministry. But I'm not suggesting we ignore the classical disciplines of seminary, only that we have a both-and approach."

"In fact, our strength at Fuller is not only our commitment to the classic theological disciplines," Richard affirmed, "but also our commitment to growing the spiritual life of the student."

Jules added, "We want to make sure the passion that students bring here will increase during seminary. Schools can very easily put a damper on the passion."

"Amen!" interjected John.

After talking to these men who are molding the minds of tomorrow's church leaders, I would affix my own concurrence.

QUESTIONS FOR GROUP STUDY

The following questions are for group study:

1. When was the last time your church leaders attended a spiritual formation and/or practical learning opportunity?
   (*a*) If this has not happened in the past six months, why not, and what should be done?
   (*b*) If it has happened in the past six months, what was the outcome?

   - Were new ideas implemented? And what were the results?
   - If not, why not?[9]

2. Compile a list of the spiritual formation and practical learning opportunities available to you. Then rate the three most effective, and attend one at the next convenient opportunity.

3. Have you investigated the latest opportunities in spiritual formation and practical learning offered by seminaries? Investigate the opportunities available. With input from your leadership team, select one opportunity for a team member to attend in the next year. Make this an annual or every-other-year event.

4. Have you recently ascertained the felt needs of your community? If not, utilize a community "Needs Assessment Survey" to uncover the topics of concern as well as the types of ministries your community residents may need.[10]

CHAPTER 10

Missteps with Small Groups

The physical presence of other Christians is a source of incomparable joy and strength to the believer.
—Dietrich Bonhoeffer, German pastor and martyr[1]

Factors That Cause Initial Growth in Churches	Erroneous Decisions That Lead to Plateauing	Corrective Steps to Regain Initial Growth
Small groups are not yet essential. The church's growth is driven by the "event status" of the celebration.	Small groups, though necessary to foster intimacy, are not sufficiently developed because the "event status" of the worship celebration continues to drive the church's emphasis and reputation. Because intimacy is missing, people feel the church is "too cold" or "not personal enough," and they go elsewhere.	Establish an extensive network of small groups to maintain intimacy and commitment as the church grows. Develop all types of small groups, including adult Sunday school classes, leadership teams, home groups, ministry groups, interest groups, organic groups, and so forth.

How Small Groups Can Be Overlooked

"We're too cold, and you can't get to know people here."

I could see a look of weariness in the pastor's face. He was the pastor of a growing church that now numbered almost six hundred. When Tom arrived at Valley Church (a pseudonym) some ten years earlier, it was a small and plateaued rural congregation. But soon its rural environs had been inundated by the suburban sprawl of a nearby city. And as a result, young families were moving to the area. Tom had slowly inaugurated change in the church that initially numbered about sixty souls. And now, some ten years later, growth had bestowed upon the congregation what Tom felt was an unwelcome appearance of success. "In our denomination everybody looks up to us as a success story," he began. "But I'm afraid if they look closer, what they'll see. We've stopped growing, and nothing seems to help."

"We built our growth on worship, prayer, and the Word," added Ryan, the minister of music. Tom continued the thought: "I knew we needed good worship to reach people today. So I made that my priority. We [nodding to Ryan] recruited musicians. As soon as we had a cohesive team of musicians, we started a new worship service." They went on to recall how the church's professional and anointed worship attracted people to the congregation. And believing that worship was one key to their growth, they added new worship services as the congregation each time filled its small sanctuary.

Effective preaching and prayer were also hallmarks. Tom had always been a good pulpiteer, able to incorporate humor and insight, both in a twenty-minute package. Prayer groups were also launched. As a result of these factors, Valley Church had grown to six hundred members.

Such success had ingratiated this church with its denomination, and it was now held up as a model of growth and renewal. "But we're not keeping near the amount of the people who visit," confided Ryan. "Our records say that we have a wide-open backdoor," added Tom. "People come, stay about a year, and then leave."

"Have you asked people why they have left?" I inquired.

"Yes," replied Ryan, "they tell us we're too cold, and you can't get to know people here."

"Small groups aren't needed here. That's for those huggy-feely churches."

Tom and Ryan described how they had tried to stem the departures by inaugurating a small group network within the church. Ryan summed up, "We know that small groups create closeness and bonding, so we started a small group ministry, but it never really took off. We've had small group nights where we invite people to join a small group. Those who attend, we divide up by geographical area and put them in short-term trial groups." Tom appraised the success of this approach, noting, "But only about fifty of more than six hundred people showed up. And only one or two groups lasted longer than a year." "We figure that less than 15 percent of our people are in small groups of any kind," concluded Ryan. "And that's not enough to keep the people who feel we're too cold."

A few minutes later Tom began to answer his own questions. In an epiphany he stated, "You know, we've never really bought into small groups enough. We haven't raised it to the level of importance that music, prayer, and preaching hold in our church. I think we've been thinking that small groups aren't needed here. That's for those huggy-feely churches."

The pastor had deftly uncovered the genesis of their malady. The congregation had focused on worship, prayer, and preaching, which had attracted people to the church. But the church had failed in elevating small groups to the level of importance and visibility that the three other ministries enjoyed. As a result, many visitors never sufficiently bonded with others in the church.

Factors That Caused Initial Growth

Here are some causes that contributed to growth at Valley Church:

Cause of Growth #1: During an early period of growth, and for a limited time, small groups were not yet essential for a church that offered attractive worship celebrations. At first, Valley Church experienced a large influx of visitors because of its reputation for anointed and modern worship. For a while, the engaging worship kept the newcomers attached, at least until they began desiring deeper interpersonal relationships among the growing assemblage of unfamiliar faces. In my observations, it is usually after the third or fourth visit that attendees begin to look for interpersonal interaction and support among a small cadre of like-minded individuals. Attendees may patiently wait up to a year and a half for the opportunity to present itself. But if these opportunities do not materialize within this window of opportunity, attendees may leave the church to look elsewhere.

While they wait, other seekers will be added to their number, and the church will grow. This continued growth misleads the leaders into thinking that small groups are not yet required to foster growth. For a short period of time they may not be. But eventually small groups are required to sufficiently attach people to a congregation. This misunderstanding is inculcated because growth is driven initially and briefly by the event status of the worship and preaching.

Cause of Growth #2: The vibrant worship and relevant music drew people into an encounter with God. Worship that ushers the participant into the presence of God cannot be stressed too highly. People today seek an encounter with the supernatural. This encounter is sometimes called by theologians the *numinous*. Philosopher Rudolf Otto pointed out that Christianity is often too influenced by what he called the "one-sided" approach of the intellect. Thus, he believed preaching and teaching may take precedence over an encounter with the supernatural. Tracing this back to the Western church's emphasis on rational thought, Otto believed churches often give people the idea that God is a "one-sided intellectualistic deity."[2]

Otto argued that humans are created with an innate desire to encounter God. Otto called this *mysterium tremendum*, or in other words, a tremendous and mysterious encounter with God. At Valley Church, an emphasis on anointed worship and prayer meant that the celebrations and prayer gatherings were venues for *mysterium tremendum* to break out. And because this need for supernatural encounter is so foundational, the rapid growth of the congregation was partially attributable to this cause.

Cause of Growth #3: An emphasis upon relevant sermons with practical "take home value" helped grow the church. Lucid and constructive teaching met another need of the congregation. When interviewed, people often remarked that a key competency of the church was that each week attendees took home some lesson or insight that they could immediately use.

Attendees relished the opportunity to feel God's presence and to hear relevant messages birthed in biblical story lines. Yet even with this connection to the supernatural, the attendees longed to be connected to each other. They wished for a deeper connection with some of the nameless faces they passed each Sunday in the foyer and aisles. The church was meeting their needs on a supernatural level, but unconsciously missing their needs on an interpersonal level.

And so, the emphasis on anointed Word, prayer, outreach, and worship grew the church. However, it was a lack of emphasis on a fifth element of sound church growth that left wide open the backdoor. The importance of attendees finding and connecting to a small group within the church was essential if attendees were to move from an audience to an army.

Why didn't the pastors notice this problem sooner?

Initially, many church leaders were involved in committees, prayer groups, and/or ministry teams, which provided the support network the leaders needed. Through the teams and committees, small groups were working behind the scenes to keep the church partially cohesive as it grew. However, similar needs of the average congregant were not as noticeable, for as the church grew, the leaders were becoming more isolated from the average attendee.

Later the next day I sat in an automotive service center. The church leaders had told me that the service manager attended Valley Church and that he seemed to be on the verge of leaving. They suggested I converse with him, and happily, the opportunity presented itself. "You go to Valley Church," I ventured.

The man's reply suggested his discomfort with the query. "Yes, along with half the people in this town," he quipped ironically. His reply gave way to a deeper discussion. Yes, he was on the verge of leaving, though he and his wife had been regular attendees for more than a year. However, they had not developed any close friendships. As our conversation closed, I asked about their future church involvement. He replied they were going to look for a small church, "where we can get to know people." As I left he offered one final observation: "But we'll miss the music and the preaching." Though attractive, even essential, the exceptional worship and teaching were not enough to overcome the couple's need to be connected.

Erroneous Decisions That Led to Plateauing

The erroneous decisions regarding small groups are some of the most enigmatic, but important.

Error 1: Leaders did not view small groups as necessary, and thus small groups were not sufficiently developed. Because the church's growth was driven by newcomers attracted to the engaging worship, the leaders did not perceive the critical nature of small groups. Because everything seemed satisfactory, the leaders had little motivation to undertake the daunting task of multiplying small groups throughout the congregation.

Error 2: The leaders were slowly distancing themselves from an understanding of the needs of their constituency. As we saw in chapter 1, when a church grows, a subtle gap may develop between the leaders and their constituency. As a result, leaders become less aware of the needs of congregants for interpersonal relationships fostered in small groups.

Error 3: The leaders were involved in small groups, sometimes informally, and thus did not feel a need to start more.

The leaders had formal, as well as informal, small groups and leadership teams that met their needs for accountability and personal interaction. Some small groups had been together since the church's inception or renewal. Because of the pressing nature of other challenges brought on by growth, and because they did not feel the need themselves, the leaders overlooked the yearning of the congregation for small group intimacy.

Error 4: Without an expansive small group network, many attendees eventually left in search of those opportunities in smaller congregations. Attendees must find and connect to a small group within the church if they are to connect with and remain in a congregation. Those who did not find a suitable small group often concluded the church was too big to offer such opportunities. Although even the largest churches can offer sufficient small group opportunities, many congregants decided this church could not. As a result, they looked toward smaller churches to meet their needs for intimacy.

Corrective Steps to Regain Growth

The Secret of Celling the Church

Small groups, sometimes called cell groups, are known to form the social and spiritual network of churches, but churches that do not foster a network of sufficient breadth will lack cohesiveness and unity. Unfortunately, an inadequate small group network often occurs in growing churches, which during periods of growth find themselves too busy to ensure their cell group network keeps pace with the increasing number of attendees. The result is that many growing churches do not connect their congregants into the life of the church, leaving an open backdoor through which many attendees exit.

What Exactly Is a Cell Group?

A cell group is generally defined as "any small group of three to twelve people formally or informally meeting approximately one or more times a month within the church fellowship network." Though it may on occasion be comprised of more than twelve individuals, the cell group's cohesiveness is rarely found in meetings of more than twenty individuals.

The "cell" designation initially stressed this group's ability to divide and multiply as it grows, in much the same manner that a human "cell" divides and multiplies. I have kept this designation because this diversifying aspect of the small group is important if the group is to avoid becoming a closed circle. Small groups should be seen as growing, living organisms that may shed dead elements and add new ones as they thrive. As the larger organism (the church) grows, the division and multiplication of cells into parallel units are important if church growth is to take place logically and coherently. For example, as a church grows, a worship committee that oversees both a traditional and a modern worship service may want to divide into two parallel committees (cells), each with responsibility over one specific worship expression. This use of parallel committees multiplies the number of small groups and defuses tension and conflict.[3]

This hiving of leadership committees is especially significant if a church is not to be hampered by a leadership structure that remains constant while the size of the congregation grows. The reader can see that "celling" leadership committees allows the church to multiply its leadership network in a fashion that keeps pace with the church's multiplication in attendees.[4]

Alternative names for cell groups. Authors have described cell groups by various other appellations. Some of the most popular include the following:

- Primary Groups (Eddie Gibbs)[5]
- Cell Groups or Kinship Circles (C. Peter Wagner)[6]
- Face-to-face Groups or Inner Fellowship Circles (Lyle Schaller)[7]

The character of cell groups. They are people centered and are characterized by intimacy and interpersonal engagement.

Examples of cell groups. They have a variety of manifestations, but fluctuate around three to twelve individuals who meet once or more a month for some of the following reasons:

- Leadership committees
- Bible studies
- Training classes
- Sunday school classes
- Classes of any kind
- Prayer groups
- Praise teams
- Any kind of church team (ministry, fellowship, and/or athletic oriented)

The function of cell groups. They may function as (but are not limited to) the following:

- Informal conclaves
- Leadership committees
- Educational opportunities (e.g., Bible studies)
- Ministry teams
- Athletic teams
- Information-gathering groups (e.g., strategy or focus groups)
- Fellowship groups
- Prayer groupings
- Regular meetings of like-minded individuals

The outcome of cell groups. Intimacy, accountability, and commitment result. People do not exit the church because they are connected with others in the congregation.

Four Steps to Celling a Church

Now that you have in mind the nature, breadth, and character of small groups, let's look at some corrective steps that can help you sufficiently expand your network to assimilate a majority of a congregation.

Corrective Step #1: Determine how many small groups you have and how many you need. Determining whether a church is healthy and capable of sustaining growth includes conducting an analysis of the number of existing small groups and adding more, if necessary. Any action that is designed to establish an adequate number of cell groups within a church I have called "celling" a church.

The general guidelines in figure 10.1 were developed to help churches determine if they have enough small groups to maintain health. These guidelines are based upon a definable "base" number: the church's average weekend celebration attendance. If a church knows this figure, it can use the guidelines to set goals that will adequately expand its cell group network.

Figure 10.1 Target Goals for Celling a Church

Column 1	Column 2	Column 3	Column 4	Column 5
Type of Small (Cell) Group:	Recommended Percentage of Average Weekend Celebration Attendance:	Target Number: The Number of Small Groups Needed. (Multiply your average weekend attendance by the percentage in column 2. Write the result here.)	Reality: The Actual Number of Small Groups. (Tally the number of groups you already have in each category.)	Goal: (Write here the number of small groups that you must *add* to reach your target number in column 3.)
Adult Sunday School Classes	4% (minimum)			
Prayer Groups	4% (minimum)			

Outreach Groups that present the good news to unchurched and dechurched people (the evangelistic mandate).	4% (minimum)			
Outreach Groups that meet the physical needs of unchurched and dechurched people (the cultural man-date).	4% (minimum)			
Worship & Celebration Groups	5% (minimum)			
Fellowship, Bible Study, and/or Home Groups. Non-Sunday morning.	6% (minimum)			
Administra-tive Leadership Groups.	8% (minimum)			
TOTALS	35% (minimum)			

How to Cell a Church: Figure 10.1 is a guide to help you set goals for the number of small groups required to adequately cell your church.

Column 1: This is a description of the type of small (cell) group under consideration.

Column 2: The church's average weekend celebration attendance will be multiplied by the percentage in column 2 to arrive at the target number (column 3). This is the typical minimum number required for church health.

Column 3: This target number is the result of multiplying the percentage in column 2 by your church's average weekend attendance. The result will be the number of small cell groups needed for a church of your size.

Column 4: In this column tally the number of small groups you already have in each category, and compare this number with the target number of column 3.

Column 5: This is your goal for the number of small groups you may need to add to make sure your church is minimally "celled."

Action Steps: To cell a church, undertake the following steps:

- Discover and define the groups that already exist in your church by using figure 10.1.
- Recommend small groups to fill each category where deficiencies lie.
- Make sure that these suggestions include the group's name, purpose, and intent.
- Implement leadership training that will provide leaders for these groups.
- Decide upon a suggested time and frequency for these small groups.
- Decide how you will assimilate the currently uninvolved segment of the congregation into these groupings.

Celling the church is not easy; it can be quite demanding. But it is of strategic importance for maintaining unity and accountability in a growing church.

Corrective Step #2: Create organic cell groups, using demographic, social, and interest data. It may be easier to "sell" the church rather than "cell" it. But celling is a price we pay for outreach and growth. It is the arduous by-product of our efforts to seek the lost. As such, it is a price a growing church must willingly pay.

A common misstep is to establish small groups around geographical zones. That happened at Valley Church. It often begins by gathering as many church attendees as possible and dividing people into groups based on geographic proximity. If there are additional divisions, they are rudimentary, usually separating people by marital status and age. Regrettably, this process is largely ineffectual in celling a sizable portion of the congregation. Geographical segregation, even when combined with marital status and age, does not usually provide enough commonality to bind people together.

The alternative is to create organic cell groups based upon a matrix of organic (or natural) commonalities. Borrowed from marketing strategies, the use of the acronym F.O.R.M. allows us to link people into more cohesive and natural groupings.[8]

F stands for *family*. Understanding someone requires knowing one's family scenario. Family status is important for helping people find the right type of cell group. Families with small children will have different needs from families with grown children (e.g., empty nesters). Single adults may have different needs from people their own age with young children. Linking people by the unique characteristics of their family structure is a starting place for designing organic cells.

O stands for *occupation*. Here we seek to link people with similar occupations. Yet now we tread on delicate ground. Occupation often tells us much about economic levels. Many times, but not always, people feel more comfortable in groups based in part on economic strata. For example, a middle manager might feel more comfortable with the owner of a small business, while an entry-level service industry employee might feel more comfortable with another person in the service sector. But categorizing people by economic strata can be abused and can be defamatory. It is best to use this category carefully. The next category, recreation, may be a better indicator of preferences and interests.

R stands for *recreation*. How a person spends leisure hours will teach you much. Most ice-breaking dialogue among unacquainted people revolves around recreation. For some, recreation may include following sporting events; for others, it may be a participatory activity such as golfing, boating, or bowling. But matching people with similar recreational habits helps link people with common interests.

M stands for the *ministry* that individuals need. This element of the acronym helps us keep in mind that people come to our churches with important needs. As we get to know people, we look for unmet needs and try to ascertain how we as a congregation can best meet them. Placing people with similar needs in a small group environment helps engender interpersonal problem solving and support.

It is simple to design a questionnaire that includes check-off options for some of these categories. For example, in a section designed to uncover a person's recreational interests there might be categories such as: bowling, watching baseball, playing baseball, playing golf, boating, fishing, playing basketball, watching basketball, scrapbooking, or gardening. Implementing such a questionnaire can help you begin to link people by their natural, or organic, commonalities.

Now, let's put all of this together so that you may match participants with an appropriate small group.

Determine potential participants' *F*, or family scenario.

Then create another subset based upon their *O* and *R* (occupation and recreational interests, respectively).

Create a further subset by looking at their *M*, or ministry they feel they need the church to provide.

In a personal interview discuss each area with the potential participant, letting each one add his or her input and adjustments.

The first three actions may be implemented through a questionnaire or an interview. However, the last action requires interpersonal dialogue and correction to allow the potential participant to help determine the organic grouping that is best for him or her. Be careful not to neglect this last action in the name of brevity.

These categories are not hard and fast. Many people will be "interest surfers," people who are technically part of one group but easily "surf" into another group, feeling at home there. The example comes to mind of a single person in his or her thirties who may feel more at home in a cell group with people the same age, but with young children. Thus, the F.O.R.M. approach is not to be implemented with an iron fist. It is a guideline to get you thinking out of the box and looking at cell group appropriateness from several different, yet organic angles.

Corrective Step #3: Consider developing a staff-level position of human resource director. Churches are discovering the benefit of designating a human resource director to oversee volunteerism and small group assimilation. In the corporate realm, a human resource director is charged with the responsibility of making the best use of the company's primary resource, its "human" resource or people. This means getting to know the workers (volunteers in the church context) and making sure they are plugged into the right jobs. A human resource director in a church can help a church accomplish the following:

- Ensure people are plugged into the right volunteer job.
- Reevaluate appropriateness and satisfaction levels of volunteers and paid staff with their duties.
- Help design and implement a congregation questionnaire designed to uncover individuals' F.O.R.M. so that they can be steered toward appropriate and cohesive groupings.
- Evaluate on a regular basis the effectiveness of the small group system's assimilation structures.
- With the church leadership, review and update the cell group system to ensure it offers the proper number and types of small groups.

Corrective Step #4: Make small groups a key part of the church personality, along with prayer, worship, outreach,

and the Word. "Word–Prayer–Outreach–Worship–Small Groups" —this healthy quintet imparts a foundation for a flourishing church. There may be other equally important elements in corporate Christian experience and growth. Leadership development, for instance, is a key, as can be seen from the emphasis I place upon it in chapters 8 and 9. But the adage "Word–Prayer–Outreach–Worship–Small Groups" addresses the central planning needs of any growing church. The use of this adage helps a church keep in perspective often overlooked planning areas that must be equally emphasized if healthy growth is to be achieved.

A SUCCESS STORY

The Meeting House, Oakville, Ontario: Where Smaller Is Better

> *"Society doesn't prepare us for small groups. Whether we are at school, a movie theater, or a sports event, our chairs always face the same direction."*

Started in 1986 as a church plant, the Meeting House had grown to 100 attendees by 1990. In those early days, current lead pastor Tim Day described the small group structure as "a typical structure where small groups are just one part of the discipleship model." Though the leaders had a vision for 1,000 attendees by the year 2000, the church had grown only to 100 in five years, which meant they were not going to meet their projections. But then something decisive happened.

Subsequently, in the year 2001, the Meeting House had attained the 1,000 mark in attendance, and in 2003 it was cracking the 2,000 mark. What energized this church's growth and transformed it from a modestly growing congregation to a surprisingly growing fellowship, doubling in size between the years 2001 and 2003?

The watershed was a message heralded by teaching pastor Bruxy Cavey. His message was simple: let's return to the Bible and take a careful look at how first-century Christians experienced discipleship and community.

One key conclusion was that the real spirit of church took

place when people turned their chairs to face each other and their shared experience of church became intimate and interactive rather than focused on one person's teaching or preaching. This, they believed, could best be experienced through small group meetings in people's homes. In response, they made these "Home Churches" a top priority. Invariably, from the pulpit you will hear it said, "The heart of the Meeting House is our Home Churches. If you have to choose between attending a Home Church and our weekend services, choose community in a Home Church." "We consider Home Churches 'real church,'" stated Tim.

"In the Bible, the vision of being a family carries the idea of having small group intimacy, interaction, and care. We see this family life as core, especially today with fragmented families. But sadly, what seems essential to the first Christ-followers is often overlooked today.

"We have discovered you have to continuously teach and reinforce this," declared Tim. "Society doesn't prepare us for small groups. Whether we are at school, a movie theater, or a sports event, our chairs always face the same direction. And this has come to be what we expect in church. But real church happens when our chairs don't face the same direction, but face each other.

"But we don't force people to join a Home Church. We regularly communicate that if you make the Meeting House your home, you will need to become a part of a Home Church to fully experience being part of this church family. If you do not, you are positioning yourself outside of our ability to care for you. And so our approach is quite simple: our weekend services are where we publicly proclaim the message of Jesus, and our Home Churches are where we help each other live it out day to day. Our goal is to be a contemporary reflection of the principles modeled in Acts 20:20.

"We need to turn up the volume on this," concluded Tim. "The starting point is not that this works as a growth strategy. The key is to remember that small, interactive groups are the essential DNA of what it means to be the reconstituted family of God. That's where we do life, where we live, where we grow in Christ. And when this happens, hey, the church grows numerically . . . just look at the book of Acts!"

QUESTIONS FOR GROUP STUDY

The following questions are for group study:

1. Fill out figure 10.1 for your church. Do you have enough small groups? In what areas are you deficient? Rank the areas that are the most critical and should be addressed first. What should be your next step to sufficiently "cell" your church? (For a reminder of the steps involved, see the action steps listed after figure 10.1.)

2. How many factors do you utilize in determining suitability of a group for a potential participant? Do you utilize demographic, social, and interest data? Take a piece of paper and divide it into three columns. Label the first column "Demographic Information," and list all of the demographic information that you could possibly discover about a person. Then do the same with columns two and three, respectively, labeling them "Social Information" and "Interest Information." Finally, circle all of the factors that you are currently using to match people to a small group. How many factors should you be utilizing? Which would be best for you to now employ? (Review the actions involved in matching participants with an appropriate small group listed in this chapter.)

3. Do you have someone functioning as a church human resource (HR) director? If not, list the duties of a HR director in the business world. Then circle the duties that could be utilized in your church. Write a job description for this church HR director. Take the job description to the appropriate committee or board, and pursue the establishment of this position.

4. "Word–Prayer–Outreach–Worship–Small Groups."
   (*a*) If you had to assign a percentage for the emphasis that each of these areas receives publicly in your church,

what ratio would you assign? Put your answer here:
_____-_____-_____-_____-_____.

(*b*) What ratio would be more appropriate for church health and growth? Put your answer here:
_____-_____-_____-_____.

(*c*) How can you reach this goal? List four steps that you could begin within thirty days to meet a balanced goal.

5. Write on a piece of paper individual words (not phrases) that describe your church. Then compare your notes with others'. What are common words that reappear? Now, ask a half dozen newcomers (who have begun attending your church in the last year) to write down words that describe your church. Compare the two lists. Where are there differences? Does small group intimacy play a bigger role in one list versus the other? If so, why do you think this is? And what is your next step? See the corrective steps in this chapter for more ideas.

CHAPTER 11

Missteps with the Centrality of Christ

Well, for us, in history where goodness is a rare pearl, he who was good almost takes precedence over he who was great.
—Victor Hugo, French poet and novelist[1]

Factors That Cause Initial Growth in Churches	Erroneous Decisions That Lead to Plateauing	Corrective Steps to Regain Initial Growth
Due to conviction, the magnitude of the task, and the potential for failure, Christ is recognized as the focal point of the church's mission and empowerment.	Along with growth comes a variety of potentials, pressures, and problems whose perceived magnitude begins to subtly dwarf the primacy of Christ.	Stay rooted in the Word, prayer, ministry, accountability, and one's mortality to keep Christ central in the lives and ministries of the congregants and leaders.

Downfall in the Foothills

"For the first time, that boy from Nebraska had respect and power, and could do what he wanted."

The senior minister of a growing church in a thriving foothill community of Los Angeles, Stewart had developed an extensive growth plan, overseen the renovation of the facility, helped triple the size of the congregation in five years—and was now leaving.

The cause of his unexpected departure was an illicit affair. "When you can't do wrong, you do wrong," were the last words he spoke to me before his departure.

Stewart was not the type of pastor one would expect to succumb to this. A pious and personable man with a loving family, he was highly regarded by colleagues both within and without his denomination. Early in his pastorate Stewart had ceaselessly pointed church and community members toward Christ as the initiator and sustainer of the church's growth. "Don't look at me," Stewart was fond of saying, "I'm just a follower like you." Stewart often led by example, eschewing his full salary in those early years to help the church meet its meager budget. "It was a time of sacrifice, stress, and coming together. It brought us to our knees in prayer," recalled Stewart.

In a phone call some five years later Stewart put the situation in perspective. "You knew I had an affair and spent money unwisely, but you didn't know why it happened," confessed Stewart. "I never thought I'd do something like that. But I changed slowly. I stopped looking to God, and started to focus on our successes. And as soon as I started to look in that direction, so did everyone else. People gave me too much credit, and I took it. For the first time, that boy from Nebraska had respect and power, and could do what he wanted. And, regrettably, I did."

I realized Stewart needed this cathartic discussion. And though it had been helpful to Stewart, it was also enlightening to me; in his story I saw how insidiously a focus on Christ can subtly shift toward self, power, influence, and sex.

Factors That Caused Initial Growth

The following only scratches the surface of the causal factors that can result in the meteoritic rise of a congregation, its reputation, and its leaders:

Cause of Growth #1: Focus was on Christ. The shepherd as well as congregation focused on what was pleasing to Christ. The critical nature of the renewal endeavor required it.

Cause of Growth #2: The congregation acknowledged Christ as the sustainer and initiator of growth. The daunting task, coupled with the insecurity of the initiators, led everyone, congregation and leaders alike, to point to God's unmistakable participation.

Cause of Growth #3: The community observed Christ as the sustainer and initiator of growth. The church's success and its utilization of inexperienced leaders fed the community's fascination with the prospect of supernatural involvement.

Cause of Growth #4: Personal preferences were surrendered for the common good. The leaders knew that for the church to survive, they must work together. And thus, unity was sought, practiced, and treasured.

Cause of Growth #5: Church growth strategies were viewed as one component in the process. Leadership strategies, gleaned from church growth and management literature, were viewed as only one element that contributed to growth.

Cause of Growth #6: There was little comfort and more tension and pressure. Growing a church is an arduous task, which often ends in failure. And in this cauldron of apprehension, tension, and insecurity the Holy Spirit is able to forge in leaders valuable character traits while keeping egos in check.

Cause of Growth #7: Prayer, Bible study, unity, and spiritual disciplines were actively practiced by the leaders. The enormity of the task drove leaders to their knees, their Bibles, their Christian friends, and reconciliation.

Erroneous Decisions That Led to Plateauing

Each of the following missteps describes how a centrality or focus on Christ was subtly replaced with a counterfeit and errant emphasis:

Error 1: Christ was replaced by power. Power is a natural by-product of responsibility, but it becomes tempting to abuse. And its use can become so intoxicating that it mars judgment. When a person who has labored for years with little real power suddenly acquires influence and authority, the result can be overwhelming and ruinous.

Error 2: Christ was replaced by success. A growing church is rare and thus noteworthy, especially for the media. This same admiration is often embraced by denominational leaders, who seek a success story to inspire other congregations. As a result, the church can begin to bask in its success and achievements. Subtly and deviously, this can steal the church's attention, time, and focus.

Error 3: Christ was replaced by personality. Related to Errors 1 and 2, leaders who navigate the precarious waters of church growth are often given too much credit for the results in lieu of the proper recipient. Again, contemporary culture and a personality-driven media can make matters worse, preferring to focus on tangible leaders rather than the Holy Spirit's unseen participation.

Error 4: Christ was replaced by money. Leaders who in the past have endured want and lack, and who are now inundated with fiscal resources, may respond chaotically, imprudently, and even selfishly. Trust in the tangible power of money may intensify, sometimes resulting in illicit procurements and expenditures.

Error 5: Christ was replaced by sex. This misdirected focus is particularly widespread due to the media's infatuation with sex to sell everything from automobiles to laundry detergent. And leaders, as well as congregants, may be drawn to the church because of feelings of powerlessness accompanied by a need to be loved. Thus, sexual interactions, even when not consummated, can become a counterfeit for the real love, empowerment, and acceptance meant to be by-products of a relationship with Christ.

Error 6: Christ was replaced by church growth principles and strategies. Euphoria often results from effective growth strategies. However, the temptation is to spend so much time lauding and studying these principles that Christ takes a backseat while church growth principles appear to drive the growth.

Error 7: Christ was replaced by exclusivity. This error occurs when congregations begin to build their focus and identity around some "special" insight or understanding they feel God has directed them to promote to the church universal. This, too, may be the outgrowth of a deficiency in power and influence that is now replaced by a special knowledge bringing prominence and influence.

Error 8: Christ was replaced by comfort. A growing church often provides increasing amounts of material goods, eminence, and influence, which in turn can lead to comfortable lifestyles. Russian playwright Anton Chekhov said, "Comfort and convenience possess a special power; little by little they suck in even people with strong wills."[2] Comfort's tendency to pacify can impede the development of valuable character traits that are engendered in challenges and difficulties. Comfort can also be one of the most insidious errors of all, for those who avoid the missteps of power, money, and sex can still easily fall prey to this malady.

Corrective Steps to Regain Growth

Six Steps to Staying Rooted in Christ

Here is a six-step prescription for keeping Christ central in the lives and ministries of both congregants and leaders:

Corrective Step #1: Stay rooted in the Word. Daily and generous doses of Bible reading and reflection are a beginning point for being grounded in servant leadership. God's Word should serve as our strategic guide (Ps. 119:105) because as Proverb 16:17 reminds us, "The highway of the upright avoids evil; he who guards his way guards his life." Allotting time for study only when preparing for sermons may rob Scripture of this meditative and regenerative power. Thus, make time for the Word in your daily schedule, your informal pursuits, your pastimes, and your plans.

Corrective Step #2: Stay rooted in prayer. Prayer should be as pervasive as study of the Word, that is, a part of your daily schedule, your informal pursuits, and so on. Eddie Gibbs calls this "respiratory prayer," for it is "the kind of regular, habitual praying that is the spiritual equivalent of breathing to sustain life."[3]

Corrective Step #3: Stay rooted in ministry. Regular participation in hands-on ministry can help thwart a misalignment of priorities. A leader who is repeatedly involved in addressing people's most basic needs, and doing so in the uncertain climate of human imperfections and sins, should strive to maintain a close link to his or her power source, God's Holy Spirit.

Corrective Step #4: Stay rooted in accountability. Some denominations utilize staff-parish committees or human resource teams to provide an accountability link between the congregation and the pastor. Other churches have denominational oversight that provides this function. However, these groups may address only skill development, overlooking spiritual development. If they do so, they abdicate half of their responsibility. And in some situations these groups may have evolved into a committee that cannot, or will not, do this. In all scenarios an accountability group is in order. Yet the discomfort of such groups often causes Christians to avoid them. Researchers Dotlich and Cairo point out, "Discomfort signals that different viewpoints are being aired . . . that teams are grappling with difficult problems in the most open ways possible."[4] The book of Proverbs confirms this, reminding us "as iron sharpens iron, so one man sharpens another" (27:17). A final excuse is that participation in an accountability group might damage a valuable personal relationship. Patrick Lencioni, author of *The Five Dysfunctions of a Team*, warns that "ironically, this only causes the relationship to deteriorate as team members begin to resent one another for not living up to expectations."[5]

Corrective Step #5: Stay rooted in your mortality. Every leader should be preparing for the day he or she passes the baton to a successor. Though you bear the baton for a while, God's picture is bigger, and one day (maybe sooner than you think) you will pass that baton. Researcher Jim Collins calls this "setting up successors for success."[6]

Corrective Step #6: Stay rooted in your priorities.
Following these steps can help a leader keep his or her priorities
aligned correctly: God, family, and ministry.

A SUCCESS STORY

Ginghamsburg United Methodist Church, Ginghamsburg, Ohio:
The Pastor's D.R.I.V.E. to Stay Focused

Ginghamsburg is the unwieldy name for an agile, fast-growing
church outside Dayton, Ohio. In the twenty years since Mike
Slaughter became senior pastor, the weekend attendance has
grown to more than 3,000, with 2,000 people involved in small
groups. Mike utilizes the metaphor of fitness to keep spiritually
rooted as the church and his responsibilities grow.

"For healthy church growth, it is critical to understand that fat
is not the same thing as fitness," Mike began. "Churches can
grow in numbers and size, but spiritual fitness takes work. It
takes sweat. The pastor really needs to work at spiritual discipline
to keep forward momentum through hard times, stale times, and
murmuring times. Just like Moses in the wilderness. And just like
an athlete in the gym.

"I use an acronym to help leaders understand how to maintain
that forward momentum. The acronym is D-R-I-V-E. It defines
the five elements that I need in my life daily.

"*D* is for personal *devotions*. This morning I was in my study
at 5:40 A.M. I spent the first hour in devotion, praying, listening
to God, along with Scripture journaling.

"*R* stands for *reading*. One of my life signature themes is learning. Thus, I have to be learning something new, and reading is
one of the best ways to do it. I read every day, and I read a diversity of things. This morning I read E. Stanley Jones, then I read
Ebony magazine to gain an understanding of one of the important
cultures represented in our church.

"*I* means I keep fit by *investing* in key relationships. This
begins with my wife and kids, and I keep them a priority. I want
them to know they are a priority even above the church. For

example, my son plays baseball on a Division 1 university team. I was gone Palm Sunday because I was with his team on the East Coast. Because there is health in my relationships, it makes my ministry healthy, too. Next, after my family, I invest in relationships with the Senior Management Team of our church. I touch base regularly with key members and leaders. I even carry a checklist to make sure I have meaningful two-way discussions with each—no one gets overlooked.

"*V* stands for *visioning*. I'm futuristic, so I constantly have to be dreaming and drawing a picture of the future. I spend time visioning every day.

"*E* is for exercise. Yesterday I was in the gym for weight training. This morning I ran for two and a half miles. Tomorrow I'll be back in the gym; Thursday I'll run. Friday and Saturday I'll be back in the gym. I like the metaphor of a gym. A gym's culture is sweat, and it takes work. People don't go to a gym for the experience; they go for the results. The church has to become more of the culture of the gym . . . a place that goes beyond experience—to results! And that means life transformation.

"If any of the letters in D-R-I-V-E are missing, I'm decelerating and not accelerating toward God's purpose. I look at life as a song of ascents . . . we should always be going upward."

QUESTIONS FOR GROUP STUDY

The following questions are for group study:

1. What topics consume most of your discussions with other leaders? What does this tell you about your priorities? Read the following scriptures, and discuss the insights that each might shed on priorities:

   - Matthew 6:25-34
   - Matthew 19:16-30
   - Mark 6:6b-13

- Luke 9:57-62
- Luke 10:1-24
- 2 Corinthians 6:3-10
- 2 Timothy 4:1-8

2. Write down the time you allot each week to

   (*a*) personal Bible study, devotionals, and reflection not related to any duties, teaching/preaching responsibilities, and so forth _____ (hours per week).
   (*b*) personal prayer _____ (hours per week).
   (*c*) personal time administrating, overseeing, and planning ministry _____ (hours per week).
   (*d*) being with family and/or close friends _____ (hours per week).
   Is there a balance? If not, what should be done?

3. How often do you participate in hands-on ministry? Would you like to do more of this? Should you? What will you do to allot adequate time?

4. Do you have an accountability group? Is it truly independent and autonomous? Is there a balance between addressing skill development and spiritual development? Why or why not? And what should be done?

5. If you were suddenly no longer available, would there be a seamless transition to your successor? If not, what should you do to set up your successor for success?

EPILOGUE

We stand in the sunrise of mission.
—Donald A. McGavran[1]

This is a quote by the visionary leader and researcher whom many call "the father of Church Growth."[2] And in the late 1970s when he looked ahead and made that remark, he could hardly have envisioned the resources the church today would have at its disposal.

Yes, the church does bask in the luminosity of potential. The future, though fraught with clashes of ideology and pedagogy, still holds great potential for the well-prepared mind. The resources, both technological and intellectual, to bring the good news to all people in understandable and logical ways have never been greater. Computers now allow us to gauge the growth and decline of corporations and, yes, even churches. And understandings of various cultural predilections and generational preferences mean we can follow Paul's example to "become all things to all men so that by all possible means I might save some" (1 Cor. 9:22). Yes, Dr. McGavran was right. We stand at the dawn of dazzling possibilities.

Yet Danish philosopher Søren Kierkegaard warned us that while we can best understand the future by looking at the past, we dare not linger too long in our annals or memoirs. Kierkegaard reminded us "that Life must be understood backwards. But that makes one forget the other saying; that it must be lived—forwards."[3] It is my hope that this book will assist church leaders in living in a forward direction, after casting a backward glance at planning missteps that have led to plateaus and/or declines in churches.

But these may be by no means all of the missteps that may be committed or encountered. These eleven are simply the most prevalent that I have witnessed in my church growth consulting practice. And thus, it is my hope that these insights give churches the needed impetus and knowledge to move forward without plateaus and regression. I also hope that this forward movement and expanding testimony will be accompanied by a deluge of God's Spirit. On the cusp of such activity, we can influence our world as never before (Acts 1:8).

Yet the strategic approach outlined in the foregoing eleven chapters may not be for everyone. Some churches will chafe at the thought of being so flexible, creative, and adaptable. But for the churches that are ready to flourish in a milieu of cultural adaptability, an understanding of the God-given factors that initially caused their growth, and an adaptation of them to their changing context, may be necessary to grow into the congregations God desires them to be.

NOTES

Introduction

1. Donald R. McGavran, *American Church Growth*, quoted in a lecture from a course taught at Fuller Seminary, 1974.

2. The following are brief descriptions of the three books in this series, designed to acquaint the reader with the significance of each book.

A House Divided: Bridging the Generation Gaps in Your Church, Bob Whitesel and Kent R. Hunter (Nashville: Abingdon Press, 2000). This first volume outlines seven steps that any church can take to reach out to young people without alienating their older members. It is the first in the "Growing a Healthy Multi-generational Church" series. "Multi-generational Church," one of many new terms introduced in this book, describes a vibrant church that is growing with attendees from all age groups. The result is a strong and vigorous church that replicates itself with younger generations.

Staying Power! Why People Leave the Church Over Change and What You Can Do About It, Bob Whitesel (Nashville: Abingdon Press, 2003). The second volume in this series describes how to defuse the tension and conflict that always arises when change is introduced. Here the reader will discover how those pressing for change often begin a six-stage leaving process if they feel they are not being heard. This book shows how to keep people who are advocating change, and then unify them with your traditional status quo members.

Growth by Accident—Death by Planning: Planning Errors That Will Kill Any Church, Bob Whitesel (Nashville: Abingdon Press, 2004). This final volume completes the cycle by providing corrective steps that will help churches that are growing sidestep the missteps that lead to plateauing in growth.

3. Initially it had been my intention to describe a direct example of a client church that succumbed to these erroneous decisions, only changing names of churches and persons. Upon review by my clients, they suggested I combine stories, while keeping the facts intact, to further protect congregational anonymity and self-esteem. In deference to my clients I have employed their suggestion.

1. Missteps with Staff Influence

1. As quoted in Brian Lanker, Barbara Sommers, and Maya Angelou, *I Dream a World: Portraits of Black Women Who Changed America* (New York: Stewart, Tabori and Chang, 1989).

2. David L. Dotlich and Peter C. Cairo, *Unnatural Leadership: Going Against Intuition and Experience to Develop Ten New Leadership Instincts* (San Francisco: Jossey-Bass, 2002), pp. 75-78.

3. Quoted by Kennon L. Callahan in *Twelve Keys to an Effective Church: Strategic Planning for Mission* (San Francisco: Harper & Row, 1983), p. xviii.

4. Gary L. McIntosh, *One Size Doesn't Fit All: Bringing Out the Best in Any Size Church* (Grand Rapids, Mich.: Fleming H. Revell, 1999), pp. 17-19.

5. Ibid., pp. 28-30.

6. In the first book of this series, *A House Divided*, I outlined how to easily launch a seven-step follow-up program for newcomers. Whitesel and Hunter, *A House Divided,* pp. 181-86.

7. Ibid., pp. 204-21.

8. In the chapter titled "Identify the Needs of the Unchurched" in *A House Divided*, I explained how to design and deploy congregational and community questionnaires that are nonobtrusive, yet reliable, pp. 141-51.

9. Again these work in both congregational and community environments, and specifics for conducting them can be found in Whitesel and Hunter, *A House Divided*, pp. 151-55.

2. Missteps with Worship Celebrations

1. William Cowper, *The Poems of William Cowper: 1782–1785,* eds. John D. Baird and Charles Ryskamp (Oxford: Claredon Press, 1996), book 2, "The Task."

2. In the second book in this series, *Staying Power: Why People Leave the Church Over Change and What You Can Do About It*, I explained why the terms "traditional, modern, and postmodern" are improved designations for describ-

ing styles of worship. "Traditional" nicely sums up liturgical styles traditionally employed because of a church's history, polity, or both. And "modern" is a better term than the oft used "contemporary" designation, since some have pointed out that our "contemporary" music is not usually contemporary, for this means "of the very latest style." Most of our contemporary music might be better described as country-rock. Thus, the term "modern," which Baby Boomers have largely accepted as a descriptor of their culture, might be better. "Postmodern" is an oxymoron that Generation X has appropriated to describe their rough-edged remaking of all things modern (and all things Boomer). And thus, it is a good label for their worship celebrations which include a fast-paced and edgy fusion of music, message, and video-clips.

3. C. Peter Wagner, *Your Church Can Be Healthy* (Nashville: Abingdon Press, 1979), pp. 88-100. Wagner tenders a very detailed exploration into the various causes of "sociological strangulation."

4. Ibid., p. 93.

5. Robert H. Schuller, *Your Church Has a Fantastic Future* (Ventura, Calif.: Regal Books, 1986), p. 246.

6. George Barna, *The Power of Vision: How You Can Capture and Apply God's Vision for Your Ministry* (Ventura, Calif.: Regal Books, 1992), p. 28.

7. Ibid., 38-39.

8. In *A House Divided* I presented eight steps for creating a vision statement. Whitesel and Hunter, *A House Divided*, p. 107.

9. Kent R. Hunter, *Your Church Has Personality: Find Your Focus—Maximize Your Mission* (Corunna, Ind.: Church Growth Center, 1997).

10. Charles Arn, *How to Start a New Service: Your Church Can Reach New People* (Grand Rapids, Mich.: Baker Books, 1997), p. 15. If you are considering starting a new service, be sure to read Arn's helpful step-by-step guide.

11. Whitesel and Hunter, *A House Divided*, "How to Identify the Needs of the Unchurched," pp. 144-60; and "The Most Popular Worship Times for Different Generations," pp. 173-76.

12. An example of a congregation that is creatively using multiple worship options is North Coast Church in Vista, California. Affiliated with the Evangelical Free Church of America, the church offers 13 worship options each weekend. All celebrations present the same teaching, either live or by video. However, worship styles vary between venues. A modern service called North Coast Live meets in the main auditorium. Three more celebrations are held in The Video Café, and each offers patio seating and flavored coffee around café tables. The Traditions Service presents live worship with a traditional flavor. And The Edge offers soft drinks along with live postmodern worship. Finally, North Coast @ Roosevelt is their off-site video venue located only minutes from the main campus at a local school. As a result, they are weekly reaching over 5,000 people.

3. Missteps with Prayer

1. Eddie Gibbs, *I Believe in Church Growth* (Grand Rapids, Mich.: William B. Eerdmans, 1981), p. 188.

2. C. Peter Wagner, *Your Spiritual Gifts Can Help Your Church Grow*, rev. ed. (Ventura, Calif.: G/L Publications, 1994), pp. 68-70, 85-86.

3. Terry Teykl, *Making Room to Pray* (Muncie, Ind.: Prayer Point Press, 1993).

4. Wagner, *Your Spiritual Gifts Can Help Your Church Grow*, p. 69.

5. Whitesel and Hunter, *A House Divided*, see especially the chapter "Step 7: Mobilizing Your Church for Transgenerational Prayer," pp. 222-37.

6. For more information on "prayer boxes" see Terry Teykl, *Box 3:16: God's Address for Hurting People* (Muncie, Ind.: Prayer Point Press, 1999).

4. Missteps with Budgets

1. The church had incorporated principles from Bob Whitesel, *Staying Power! Why People Leave the Church Over Change and What You Can Do About It* (Nashville: Abingdon Press, 2003).

2. Jim Collins, *Good to Great: Why Some Companies Make the Leap ... and Others Don't* (New York: Harper Collins Publishers, 2001), p. 125.

3. Aaron Wildavsky, *The New Politics of the Budgetary Process*, 4th edition (Glenview, Ill.: Scott Foresman & Co, 1998), p. 1.

4. Ibid., p. 2.

5. Ibid., pp. 2-3.

6. Fred. R. David, *Strategic Management: Concepts and Cases* (Upper Saddle River, N.J.: Prentice Hall, 2001), pp. 287-88.

5. Missteps with New Facilities

1. Winston Churchill, *Time* (New York, September 12, 1960).

2. For ideas on "unity celebrations" that can unify churches with multiple weekend worship options, see "Unity Building Exercises" in Whitesel and Hunter, *A House Divided*, p. 187.

3. See the second book in this series, *Staying Power: Why People Leave the Church Over Change and What You Can Do About It*, to discover how to keep your people from coalescing into factions.

4. Robert H. Schuller, *Your Church Has a Fantastic Future* (Ventura, Calif.: Regal Books, 1986), p. 286.

5. In the second book of this series, *Staying Power: Why People Leave the Church Over Change and What You Can Do About It*, I explained how you can avoid the polarization that often arises between these groups.

6. David Price of ChurchWorks Architects/Builders is one of the most creative minds in church architecture and church design. Visit his website at www.dapassoc.com for more information about the next generation of church design.

7. For a step-by-step guide to computing your "Average Annual Growth Rate (AAGR)" see figure 10:5 in *A House Divided*, pp. 216-18.

8. The second volume in this series, *Staying Power*, describes ways to diffuse this polarization.

6. Missteps with Innovation

1. Alexis de Tocqueville, *Democracy in America*, ed. Harvey C. Mansfield, trans. Debra Winthrop (Chicago: University of Chicago Press, 2000), vol. 2, pt. 3, ch. 21.

2. See chapter 2 if you need to review the nature of "philosophy of ministry" or personality statements.

3. Effective strategies should be consistent with a philosophy of ministry statement. But still there remains leeway to creatively vary your ministries and keep them consistent with your church personality. For example, a church whose strength is in music ministry may decide to attract younger community residents by launching praise teams in addition to choirs. In this example, the church would still be staying with one of its strengths (quality and anointed music), but through experimentation it is embracing modern forms that can reach younger community residents. Hence, creativity and variety is engendered while maintaining consistency with the church's personality.

4. For an in-depth discussion see Eddie Gibbs, *I Believe in Church Growth* (Grand Rapids, Mich.: William B. Eerdmans Publishing Co., 1981), chapter 5, "Medium and Message," pp. 187-233.

5. A contributing factor is that if an unchurched or dechurched person has a negative experience with a ministry, he or she may avoid that ministry in the future. And thus, the unchanging message may be evaded because the medium through which it is presented did not adapt. Presenting the good news in creative new forms, without compromising values or theology, requires the unchurched and dechurched person to wrestle anew with biblical implications.

6. Daniel Boorstin, *The Americans: The Democratic Experience* (New York: Vintage, 1974), p. 369.

7. Herb Miller, *How to Build a Magnetic Church*, Creative Leadership Series, ed. Lyle E. Schaller (Nashville: Abingdon Press, 1987), pp. 119-20.

8. Peter F. Drucker, "The Discipline of Innovation," *Harvard Business Review* (Boston: Harvard Business School Publishing, 1985, reprint 2002), vol. 6, no. 6, p. 149.

9. Miguel de Cervantes Saavedra, *Don Quixote* (New York: W. W. Norton & Company, 1981), Part i. Book iv. Chap. iv.

10. L. G. Franko, "Global Corporate Competition: Who's Winning, Who's Losing, and the R&D Factor as One Reason Why," *Strategic Management Journal* (New York: John Wiley & Sons, 1989), no. 10, pp. 449-74.

11. Dotlich and Cairo, *Unnatural Leadership: Going Against Intuition and Experience to Develop Ten New Leadership Instincts*, pp. 245-46.

12. Quoted in Walter G. Bennis and Robert J. Thomas, *Geeks and Geezers:*

How Era, Values, and Defining Moments Shape Leaders (Boston: Harvard Business School Press, 2002), pp. 101-2.

13. David S. Landes, *The Wealth and Poverty of Nations: Why Some Are So Rich and Some So Poor* (New York: W. W. Norton and Company, 1998), p. 200. Jim Collins in *Good to Great* describes further how buildup and breakthrough creates new options.

14. Gareth R. Jones, Jennifer M. George, and Charles W. L. Hill, *Contemporary Management*, 2nd ed. (Boston: Irwin, McGraw-Hill, 2000), p. 217.

15. Ibid.

16. Debra L. Nelson and James Campbell Quick, *Organizational Behavior: Foundations, Realities, and Challenges*, 3rd ed. (Cincinnati: South-Western Publishing, 2000), pp. 333-34.

17. Quoted by Sy Landau, Barbara Landau, and Daryl Landau in *From Conflict to Creativity: How Resolving Workplace Disagreements Can Inspire Innovation and Productivity* (San Francisco: Jossey-Bass, 2001), p. 109.

18. A. F. Osborn, *Applied Imagination: Principles and Procedures of Creative Problem Solving* (New York: Scribner Publishers, 1963), p. 149.

19. Sy Landau, Barbara Landau, and Daryl Landau in *From Conflict to Creativity: How Resolving Workplace Disagreements Can Inspire Innovation and Productivity*, pp. 128-29.

20. Gareth R. Jones, Jennifer M. George, and Charles W. L. Hill, *Contemporary Management*, p. 218.

21. W. H. Cooper, R. B. Gallupe, S. Pollard, and J. Cadsby, "Some Liberating Effects of Anonymous Electronic Brainstorming," *Small Group Research* (Thousand Oaks, Calif.: Sage Publications, 1998), pp. 147-78.

22. D. H. Gustafson, R. K. Shulka, A. Delbecq, and W. G. Walster, "A Comparative Study of Differences in Subjective Likelihood Estimates Made by Individuals, Interacting Groups, Delphi Groups, and Nominative Groups," *Organizational Behavior and Human Performance* (New York: Academic Press, 1973), no. 9, pp. 280-91.

23. Peter Block, *The Answer to How Is Yes* (San Francisco: Berrett-Koehler Publishers, 2002), p. 162.

24. Walter G. Bennis and Robert J. Thomas, *Geeks and Geezers: How Era, Values, and Defining Moments Shape Leaders*, p. 104.

25. *New York Times*, February 18, 1994.

26. Adapted from Dotlich and Cairo, *Unnatural Leadership: Going Against Intuition and Experience to Develop Ten New Leadership Instincts*, pp. 82-83.

7. Missteps with Evaluation

1. Quoted in Fred R. David, *Strategic Management*, 8th ed. (Upper Saddle River, N.J.: Prentice Hall, 2001), p. 301.

2. For information on how to prevent information cascades from polarizing a

congregation, see Bob Whitesel, *Staying Power: Why People Leave the Church Over Change.*

3. For more on "information cascades," see Felix Oberholzer-Gee, "Learners or Lemmings: The Nature of Information Cascades," in Stephen J. Hoch, Howard C. Kunreuther, with Robert E. Gunther, ed., *Wharton on Making Decisions* (New York, John Wiley and Sons, 2001), pp. 273-86.

4. Harvey Mackay, *Swim with the Sharks Without Being Eaten* (New York: Ivy Books, 1988), pp. 137-39.

5. Ibid., p. 138.

6. In the first volume of this series I described a seven-step process for assimilating your newcomers. Whitesel and Hunter, *A House Divided*, pp. 181-86.

7. David Dotlich and Peter Cairo, *Unnatural Leadership: Going Against Intuition and Experience to Develop Ten New Leadership Instincts* (San Francisco: Jossey-Bass, 2002), p. 81.

8. In the first book of this series I showed how counting is a time-honored biblical practice. Whitesel and Hunter, *A House Divided*, p. 206.

9. Whitesel and Hunter, *A House Divided*, chapter 10: "Step Six: Evaluate Your Success," pp. 202-21. Here you will find six charts that will help you measure the four types of church growth found in Acts 2:42-47.

10. In the first book I show how to gauge maturation growth with a helpful "Composite Maturation Number" calculated from attendance in learning activities (such as Sunday school classes, Bible studies, etc.) and weekend worship attendance. Whitesel and Hunter, *A House Divided*, pp. 207-9.

11. Ibid., p. 205.

12. In *Good to Great: Why Some Companies Make the Leap ... and Others Don't*, p. 139, researcher Jim Collins discovered that successful companies have "stop doing" lists in addition to "to do" lists. Collins muses, "most of us lead busy but undisciplined lives. We have ever-expanding 'to do' lists, trying to build momentum by doing, doing, doing—and doing more. And it rarely works. Those who build the good-to-great companies, however made as much use of 'stop doing' lists as 'to do' lists."

13. Personal email to the author, dated January 7, 2003.

8. Missteps with Dysfunctional People

1. Donald A. McGavran, *Understanding Church Growth,* rev. ed. (Grand Rapids, Mich.: Eerdmans Publishing Co., 1980), p. 313.

2. Ibid., pp. 295-313. McGavran warns that church growth can halt when "redemption and lift" increases the distance between maturing disciples and their former associates. For an in-depth look at how to prevent the halting of growth, consult McGavran's exhaustive study.

3. This triangle is based in part on the research of Stephen B. Karpman. However, while Karpman's Triangle looks at how an individual can mutate

between rescuer—persecutor—victim, the triangles I propose illustrate how victims perceive and react toward those who reach out to them.

4. Pete Scazzero, *The Emotionally Healthy Church* (Grand Rapids, Mich.: Zondervan, 2003). This is one of the best books available for developing the emotional life of the leader. Read this book early on in your leadership training.

9. Missteps with Staff Education

1. Alexander Isaevich Solzhenitsyn, *The Oak and the Calf* (New York: Harper & Row, 1981), p. 80.

2. For an exhaustive numerical comparison of the effects of education, practical experience, and spiritual formation on church growth see Roger Finke and Rodney Stark, *The Churching of America 1776–1990: Winners and Losers in Our Religious Economy* (New Brunswick, N.J.: Rutgers University Press, 2000), and Roger Finke and Kevin Dougherty, "The Effects of Professional Training: The Social and Religious Capital Acquired in Seminaries," in *Journal for Scientific Study of Religion* 41 (2002): 103-20.

3. Finke and Dougherty, "The Effects of Professional Training," pp. 112-13.

4. Seminaries known to the author that are endeavoring to balance spiritual formation and practical learning are (in alphabetical order): Asbury Seminary, Kentucky; Denver Seminary, Colorado; Fuller Seminary, California; George Fox Evangelical Seminary, Oregon; Golden Gate Seminary, California; Mid-America Baptist Seminary, Tennessee; Southern Baptist Theological Seminary, Kentucky; Talbot Seminary, California; Trinity Seminary, Illinois; among others.

5. Conrad Cherry, *Hurrying Toward Zion: Universities, Divinity Schools, and American Protestantism* (Bloomington: Indiana University Press), p. 38.

6. H. Richard Niebuhr, with Daniel Day Williams and James M. Gustafson, *The Purpose of the Church and Its Ministry* (New York: Harper Publishing, 1956), pp. 110, 130.

7. This is another example of the impact of what McGavran calls "redemption and lift," *Understanding Church Growth*, pp. 295-313.

8. Finke and Dougherty, "The Effects of Professional Training," pp. 112-13.

9. Bob Whitesel, *Staying Power*. As the second part in this series, this book lays down foundational principles and steps that are valuable in effectively deploying the strategies of this current book.

10. Bob Whitesel and Kent Hunter, *A House Divided*, pp. 144-60.

10. Missteps with Small Groups

1. Dietrich Bonhoeffer, *Life Together*, trans. John W. Doberstein (New York: Harper, 1954), p. 19.

2. Rudolf Otto, *The Idea of the Holy*, trans. John W. Harvey, 2nd ed. (New York: Oxford University Press, 1950), p. 3.

3. In the first book of this series, *A House Divided*, I examined parallel committees at length in the chapter titled, "Leading the Multi-generational Church." Using charts and graphs, I demonstrated how a growing church can divide its leadership committees into parallel cells as growth in the congregation occurs. Whitesel and Hunter, *A House Divided*, pp. 121-43.

4. Some may wonder if organizational cohesiveness can be preserved when leadership cells (i.e., committees) divide as the church, and leadership duties grow. However, unity is preserved among parallel committees by establishing "executive committees" comprised of representatives of the parallel committees they oversee. These "executive committees" serve as oversight committees to the parallel committees below them, working out conflict and reporting to committees above them regarding the work of the parallel committees.

An example would be a church with three different worship celebrations. The traditional service would receive oversight from the "Traditional Worship Committee." Parallel to this committee, and overseeing the modern celebration would be a "Modern Worship Committee." Likewise over a Gen. X and postmodern worship celebration would be the "Postmodern Worship Committee." Of course these names might change based upon each church's predilections and preferences. But here they serve as examples.

An "Executive Worship Committee" is then comprised of two representatives from each of these three committees. This executive committee would be responsible for working out conflicts between the three worship committees, such as facility usage, equipment sharing, timing, and so forth. The executive committee would also report to the church administrative body the workings of the three worship celebrations.

5. Eddie Gibbs, *I Believe in Church Growth* (Grand Rapids, Mich.: Eerdmans Publishing Company, 1981), p. 276.

6. C. Peter Wagner, *Your Church Can Grow* (Glendale, Calif.: G/L Publications, 1976), pp. 107-8.

7. Lyle E. Schaller, *Effective Church Planning* (Nashville: Abingdon, 1981), pp. 17-63, and *Growing Plans: Strategies to Increase Your Church's Membership* (Nashville: Abingdon, 1983), pp. 91-94.

8. Whitesel and Hunter, *A House Divided*, pp. 180-81.

11. Missteps with the Centrality of Christ

1. Victor Hugo, *Les Misérables*, trans. William G. Allen (New York: Schoenhofs Foreign Books, 1997).

2. Anton Pavlovich Chekhov, *My Life, Works* (New York: Harcourt & Brace 1976), vol. 9, p. 228.

3. Eddie Gibbs, *Church Next: Quantum Changes in How We Do Ministry* (Downers Grove, Ill.: InterVarsity Press, 2000), p. 135.

4. Dotlich and Cairo, *Unnatural Leadership: Going Against Intuition and Experience to Develop Ten New Leadership Instincts,* pp. 141-42.

5. Patrick Lencioni, *The Five Dysfunctions of a Team* (San Francisco: Jossey-Bass, 2002), p. 213.

6. Jim Collins, *Good to Great: Why Some Companies Make the Leap ... and Others Don't,* pp. 25-27.

Epilogue

1. *The Church Growth Bulletin* (Pasadena, Calif.) March 1978, Vol. XIV, No. 4, p. 191. Additionally, in *Church Growth State of the Art* (Wheaton, Ill.: Tyndale House, 1986), p. 15, C. Peter Wagner calls this quote "perhaps the most characteristic phrase proclaimed through the years by Donald A. McGavran, regarded by many as the twentieth century's premier missiologist."

2. Wagner, *Church Growth State of the Art*, p. 15.

3. Søren Kierkegaard, *The Diary of Søren Kierkegaard*, ed. Peter P. Rohde (New York: Citadel Press, 1960), p. 111.